THE COMMUNION RITE AT SUNDAY MASS

THE

COMMUNION RITE
AT SUNDAY MASS

Gabe Huck

LTP

LITURGY TRAINING PUBLICATIONS

ACKNOWLEDGMENTS

This book is both a narrative about the communion rite and a collection of many good things that have been written about this rite. These words are enriched with many photos. I am grateful to the photographers and to the publishers of those materials that are used here by permission. My thanks especially to the Liturgical Conference whose book, *It Is Your Own Mystery*, covered much of this ground in a most wonderful way in 1977. That book is now out of print; those fortunate enough to possess a copy should know it as a continuing source of wisdom and direction.

Some of the supplementary materials in these pages may be reprinted for use in parishes without further permission from Liturgy Training Publications. These texts contain the LTP copyright notice; that notice should be retained on all reproductions. Other materials may be reproduced only with permission from LTP or, in the case of some of the supplementary materials, the copyright owner.

Gabe Huck

Photographs by James Liebner, SVD: pages 19, 23, 28, 45, 49, 53, 61, 63, 65, 91
Photographs by Phyllis Fahrer: pages 15, 81
Photographs by Mary Beth Campbell: pages 31, 36, 83, 87
Bulletin insert art by Barbara Schmich.
Cover and book design by Jane Kremsreiter.
Page makeup by Mark Hollopeter.

ISBN 0-930467-91-4

Printed in the United States of America.

CONTENTS

Titles of supplementary materials are noted in italics.

51 THE COMMUNION PROCESSION

89 THE PRAYER AFTER COMMUNION

93 AFTERWORD

95 APPENDIX

THIS BOOK is about *the communion rite.* It is about everything that happens after the Amen of the eucharistic prayer and before the announcements and final blessing. That is the communion rite: the Lord's Prayer, the peace greeting, the breaking of the bread, the communion procession, the prayer after communion. We will discuss this as a rite, a ritual done by the church. We will discuss the way this rite can best be done. It is not a book of theology, but a practical book for those who prepare the liturgy.

This book is about the communion rite *at Mass.* It is not, therefore, about the communion rite when it is celebrated in any other setting, such as communion of the sick or a communion service following the liturgy of the word.

This book is about the communion rite at *Sunday* Mass. Some things that are said here will apply to weekday Masses, but Sunday Mass is always being directly addressed in these pages. Sunday is the Lord's Day, the day that Christians took to themselves from their very first generations. From that time on it has been marked with an assembly, and the work of that assembly has been the eucharist. It is especially important in these times, when we hear of the decreasing number of ordained ministers, to recall that "eucharist" here does not mean simply holy communion. Sunday Mass is not holy communion. It is eucharist. It is what we do before communion as well as in the communion rite.

Eucharist means the "giving thanks and praise" that is done in the eucharistic prayer. This act, this summing up of all our prayer and all our living, flows into the communion rite. But there is a vast difference between this eucharist and a liturgy of holy communion when there is no eucharistic prayer and everyone receives the bread reserved beforehand. The former is what Christians have come together to do on the Lord's Day. The latter is a stopgap measure—like communion in time of persecution. It is done only when there cannot be a eucharist. A Sunday communion service, a Sunday therefore without the eucharist, is contrary to all the centuries of Catholic practice. Although this book will not be dealing with the eucharistic prayer as such, it must be established at the beginning that without the strongest efforts to make the eucharistic prayer look and sound and feel like the heart of our liturgy, there is hardly any point in trying to do the communion rite well.

This book is about the communion rite at Sunday Mass *in the parish*. Our eucharist is always the eucharist of the church. It has no existence apart from the celebration of particular assemblies. For us, these assemblies are our parishes, places where baptized Catholics have bound themselves to one another and to the local bishop. The bishop is

Catechesis and Sunday Eucharist

On the first day of Lent in 1980, Pope John Paul wrote a letter to bishops and clergy on the "Mystery and Worship of the Most Holy Eucharist." During the course of his reflection he drew their attention to a phenomenon that, in his judgment, calls for widespread pastoral attention and even the analysis of theologians. What worried him? "Sometimes, indeed quite frequently, everybody participating in the eucharist goes to communion."

What are we to make of his questioning this fact? So much official effort has been expended during this century to get the people to understand that their participation in Sunday Mass is incomplete unless they share in the meal. People everywhere seemed to get the point. Now not only do we have large numbers of communicants every Sunday, we have laity ministering the eucharist to the laity as a quite normal practice. We have reason to ask what is behind Pope John Paul's concern? If we let him speak for himself, he proposes "the good quality of sensitiveness of Christian conscience" as a precondition for making a judgment about coming forward to communion.

both symbol of our unity in Christ and our bond with the church throughout the world and through the centuries. At Sunday liturgy the one who presides is one whom our bishop has delegated: The pastor stands in the bishop's place and presides at the eucharist of this particular church. That is our Catholic way of doing things—Sunday, assembly of the baptized, eucharist with the bishop or the bishop's delegate.

This is the home of the communion rite. This is where we get to know what it means and what it takes.

WHAT DOES THE COMMUNION RITE LOOK LIKE?

Why all the fuss? After all, it seems pretty straightforward. Everyone says the Our Father and shakes a few hands when the invitation is given. When the communion ministers are ready, the ushers let people come forward row by row to receive communion. Afterward, the presider reads the prayer after communion.

But one could also describe the communion rite this way: It happens only after we have come together with singing and the sign of the cross and prayer, after we have attended to God's word read out in our

In his letter the Pope reflected at some length on the sensitiveness of conscience that supports an authentic sense of the eucharist. He wrote, "If our eucharist is authentic, it must make us grow in the awareness of the dignity of each person. The awareness of that dignity becomes the deepest motive of our relationship with our neighbor." He makes the challenge to the sensitivity of the Christian conscience more concrete when he continues, "We must become particularly sensitive to all human suffering and misery, to all injustice and wrong, and seek the way to redress them effectively." Put quite plainly, Pope John Paul II is concerned: Do we who now come so easily to the eucharistic table every Sunday have a significant realization of the broad ethical implications of our decision to take and eat of the body and blood of the Lord Jesus?

Catechists are orienting both adults and children into the life of Catholic faith and practice. They undoubtedly intend to bring to those they instruct the rich tradition of the universal church. Yet each of us is fixed in time and place. Inevitably we hand on the faith of the church as we have received it, made sense of it and appropriated it for our own lives. We need to encourage each other to become a little more critical of the ways in which we ourselves have so far appropriated the eucharistic faith of the church and now hand it on. We must think

midst and to the preaching, after we have joined in a litany of intercession for the world and the church, and, most of all, after we have lifted our hearts to the Lord in praise and thanks and strong acclamation of the eucharistic prayer.

We probably pause when that Amen is finished. Something has ended. People shift around a little bit. We find ourselves standing together around the altar. On it are the bread and wine become for us the body and blood of our Lord. Together we pray the Lord's Prayer. Everyone knows it, the summation of all our prayers, and it sounds sturdy. Then, at the invitation of the deacon, the words "peace" and "Christ's peace" flow through the assembly as people embrace or join hands: family, acquaintances, strangers, young and old, those with much in common and those with nothing in common—except baptism, and that is far more than anything that divides.

further about the kind of life which is a necessary counterpart of regular eucharistic communion at Sunday Mass, a necessary counterpart of any reliable eucharistic catechesis. We need to think again, as Catholics living at the end of the 20th century, about an authentic understanding of participation in the eucharist.

Getting American Catholics who come to Mass to receive communion is relatively easy. That has been accomplished by papal decrees, the work of earlier generations of pastors and catechists and finally by the liturgical reforms of Vatican II.

But have we risen to the occasion? The very question may now catch us off guard, as it did the hapless wedding guest of the parable (Matthew 22:12) who, when questioned about why he had come not properly dressed, had nothing to say. Do we even know what rising to the occasion means? In thinking about this, we may continue to take our lead from Pope John Paul's own reflections in that 1980 letter, provided that we are willing to probe his language. In the letter he wrote, "The eucharist is, above all else, a sacrifice."

Sacrifice is a term loaded with the freight of centuries. We nod, "above all else, a sacrifice," but having said that, we have not really clarified anything. We must begin by acknowledging that, for those who follow Jesus, authentic sacrifice is not a matter of "someone else must die so that I can live." Sacrifice is rather the gift of my life for the life of the world. Sacrifice in the model Jesus proposes means, "I spend myself so that others may live."

This idea does not sell well as good news. Such is the sacrificial crisis that the church faces today: baptized Christians who are not committed to continuing the sacrifice of Jesus—giving their lives for the life of the world—but who come in long lines to communion anyway. It is not necessarily the case that our kind come in bad faith, but we come naively.

The Rite within the Mass

The noise and motion subside as the presider silently lifts up a large loaf of bread and breaks it. Now the communion is being prepared: Others come forward and assist the presider and the deacon as the bread is broken into small pieces and the wine is poured into cups. For as long as this takes, the cantor sings the Lamb of God in a back-and-forth style with the assembly. This is a litany in which we pray again and again for God's mercy. As we sing, a procession begins to form. The communion ministers are coming toward the assembly with plates and cups, the assembly is beginning the communion procession. The litany ends and the presider speaks the invitation: "This is the Lamb of God. . . . Happy are those who are called . . ." Everyone responds "Lord, I am not worthy."

Then the communion procession moves through the room. It is a procession of people who join in singing the refrains of psalms and other songs or in chanting simple verses over and over again. Each one stands

The early Christians' names for this corporate action were "the breaking of the bread" and "thanksgiving." The names simply described one or the other aspect of their behavior during their gathering: They broke bread, they gave thanks. The judgment that this activity could be called sacrifice was sparked by somebody's capacity to see connections, to arrive at some insight. What was connecting? Three things, all of them familiar and all of them clustering together in a new pattern of religious meaning.

The first of these three was the awareness of the great deed of Jesus' own life and his death, an awareness alive in the community and recorded in the scriptures read in their liturgical assemblies. Attending to the reality of Jesus over and over again, believers became increasingly more certain that Jesus had personally embodied and lived out the mysterious plan of God for the world's salvation. The traditional temple program of offering sacrifices for sin and sacrifices of thanksgiving was in-creasingly irrelevant. Their first insight was this: The old sacrifices which were offered daily to take away the sins of the world were well-intentioned, but here is the one who takes away the sin of the world by the truth of his life. If you want to know what God is doing to save the world, keep your eye on Jesus. Despite opposition, even when threatened with death, he cared for the sick and the poor, drove out the demons which obsessed people, forgave sins, taught his disciples to imitate him. He is the only sacrifice necessary. That is the truth.

The second realm of insight came with reflection on their own discipleship. They followed Jesus, living as he did: forgiving their enemies, serving the poor, proclaiming liberty to captives, praising God and giving thanks for the gift of Jesus to the world. Thus their lives were in some way an extension of his. They were the body of Christ. He was the head, they the members. Their lives joined to his were glorifying God and overcoming sin. So the second

before the communion ministers, is addressed with "The body of Christ," "The blood of Christ," and responds "Amen." The procession and its singing conclude as the vessels are carried to a table on the side. There is stillness, then, as movement and sound cease for a while. Then the presider speaks the prayer after communion.

What follows is blessing and sending forth, taking leave of one another, often with song.

HOW TO THINK ABOUT RITUAL

Sometimes we think of the Sunday liturgy as just one little item after another. But it is far from that. It is, first of all, the joining of two major rituals, one centered on the word and the other on the

---

insight was this: Vigorous Christian life has the same power (the Holy Spirit) and the same effect (glorifying God, overcoming sin) as the sacrifice of Jesus. In him, we are living sacrifices.

The final connection was inevitable. When living sacrifices named Ignatius, Agatha, Cecilia, Justin gathered in the name of Jesus to remember the paradoxical sacrifice of his life, the symbolic celebration of his sacrifice and theirs was—what else?—a sacramental sacrifice. The human event was recognized and celebrated as a sacred event. If the eucharist is, above all else, a sacrifice, it is so as the symbolic, sacramental meeting place for the two living sacrifices. The truth of Jesus' self-gift for the life of the world is not in question. But that is not the whole truth of the eucharist as sacrifice according to the original insight.

If the truth is that the "eucharist is, above all else, a sacrifice," the whole truth is that it takes two— Christ and the church—to have that sacrifice sacramentally present.

With this insight, we can understand the Pope's concern. What if one of the two doesn't meet the precondition for the eucharistic meal, namely, that it is a celebration of a living sacrifice? What if the church comes unprepared for the occasion? Pastors have long had to worry about this question. It represents a chronic problem which becomes acute in times of change. In the third century, the North African bishop, Cyprian, once wrote to reprimand a wealthy woman in his church who made no offering of her resources for the care of the poor but who presumed nevertheless to show up at the communion table. From Cyprian's perspective, the poor and rich alike must spend themselves for others. This is the concrete self-gift of the church, the gift celebrated in the eucharist. The wealthy woman who refused her gift was denying—even mocking—the truth of the eucharist. The eucharist is, above all else, a sacrifice: yours—joined to Christ's.

Excerpts from "Catechesis and Sunday Eucharist," by Mary Collins. Reprinted from *Liturgy 80*, April 1982, pp. 2–7.

eucharist. Before the book is opened for that liturgy of the word, however, there are rites of assembling: song and greeting, praise and prayer. And after the eucharist is concluded, there are rites of taking leave: announcements and blessings and song.

The liturgy of the word also has its own movement. It is not some arbitrary ordering of readings and psalms and processions and homilies, but a well-worn pattern by which we publicly proclaim and give attention to our scriptures. And the liturgy of the eucharist—beginning with the preparation of the table and the gifts—has its own dynamic: the quiet table preparation followed by the call to lift up our hearts in the central prayer of praise and thanksgiving, a prayer that is punctuated by songs of acclamation. The communion rite follows as the Lord's Prayer and peace greeting lead to communion itself.

Not a random series of little rites at all, the Mass is this meeting of two liturgies—word and eucharist—with brief rites of entrance and dismissal. But it can feel random when it seems to belong to somebody else, when we seem to be an audience. The flow of these moments, their power and their capacity to catch us up and give shape to our lives, is a matter of conviction and hard work, discipline and education, practice and common sense. It can come about in any parish willing to embark on such a task.

The reform of the liturgy in the past decades has been primarily about one thing: restoring liturgy to the people so that it can be the source of our lives. For this to happen, the liturgy cannot be something we "attend," but something we know well how to do. Its movement has to get into our bones. The basic shape of our liturgy we receive from the tradition. We place something of ourselves upon this and then we hand it on to our children.

DOING WHAT IS OURS TO DO

*T*he reform has been long in coming and slow in taking root. It could hardly be otherwise. We are challenged to do the liturgy with a zeal and involvement not asked or allowed for centuries. That's hard, and made harder by two other factors.

First, many are afraid that the reform has taken all the beauty and mystery from their liturgy. It need not and in the long run it will not, but often, in practice, it has. The deeds of our liturgy—scripture read aloud, psalms sung, homilies preached, litanies chanted, God praised for all gifts over the bread and wine, greetings of peace, holy communion— these are capable of great beauty and wonder, Sunday after Sunday. But the mystery is not simply to be passively taken in. It now demands engagement, demands preparation (of heart and body as well as of book and bread), demands care and attention from everybody.

The second thing that has made the reform difficult is something about our times and our place. Life in the late 20th century in the United States doesn't prepare us to be doers of the liturgy. Rather, we are treated from morning until night as an audience, often as an audience of consumers. Products, entertainment, the news—everything is packaged for an audience. And we come to the liturgy well-trained in being an audience. That's what we expect, what we do well. Knowing that, those who prepare the liturgy have at times been satisfied to let the congregation be an audience, and we have acted like an audience: We're there to "get something out of liturgy," to leave feeling a little better, to get a lift or an insight, to help us cope with the week.

All that has been off the mark of liturgical renewal. What is slowly emerging, here and there, is a liturgy that doesn't set out to entertain or educate or inspire, but rather to be in the hands of the baptized people who come on Sunday. That never means that our liturgy is whatever people vote for. The liturgy is what we have received, what we hold (but do not really own) and shape a bit to our times and then hand on.

Nowhere in the liturgy is this relationship of the baptized people to their liturgy as clear as it is in the communion rite. In the liturgy of the word, there is much back and forth between lectors and cantor and homilist and assembly. During the eucharistic prayer, the presider and the assembly take vital roles of proclamation and acclamation. But when we come to the communion rite, it is as if the assembly is now the protagonist. The presider says very little, just words of invitation and a few short prayers. The cantor and other musicians facilitate the singing of the assembly. Ushers and communion ministers perform services for the assembly in the communion procession. But for all these ministries, it is the assembly that is acting. Who prays the Lord's Prayer? Who does the peace greeting? Who chants the Lamb of God litany? Who makes up the communion procession? Who sings? Who keeps silence afterward and then attends to the final prayer?

The communion rite is the assembly doing what a Catholic assembly is meant to do. It is what we have done so well that we are freed from looking at directions in books, freed from page turning or spoken signals, freed to enter fully into the meaning of these words and movements and deeds. Prayers and litanies and songs are ours to do. Processing is ours. Eating and drinking the body and blood of Christ is above all ours to do. We are in fact getting into our whole being what is the stuff and the shape of a Catholic life.

The urgency of a parish communion practice on Sundays that allows all this to happen is not for the sake of some aesthetic notion of good liturgy, nor merely to follow the rubrics, though it is both these things. It is about giving to the assembly what is theirs, giving to baptized people the rituals to which baptism entitles them. It is impossible to put this on paper. It is something people do. Learning about it comes from being one of those people—and not just once, but Sunday after Sunday. The task of those who have responsibility for parish liturgy, of people who would be studying this book, is to enable such a transformation to happen. The work is to prepare ministers, to prepare the objects and the environment and to challenge and invite the assembly to a habitual way of doing this rite. That "way" will be what they know how to do and—it is hard to imagine but very possible—what they hunger and thirst to do.

USING THIS BOOK

When we would speak about the communion rite (or about any single part of the liturgy), we survey the moments of this rite, seeing how they are sometimes misunderstood and misused, and we try to imagine and discuss what the rite should look and sound like.

That is what we shall offer in these pages: a straightforward discussion of the communion rite accompanied by a wealth of special materials, gathered from various sources, to bring insight and/or practical help. To make full use of this book, attend to all these elements.

THE RITE AS A WHOLE

The sections that follow deal individually with the moments of the communion rite. This seems the only practical approach. It should not obscure in any way the unity of this rite, the flow between these moments. For all practical purposes, the person taking part should

---

How Do We Fashion and Revere the Cup?

The chalice and the paten—words coming from the Latin and meaning a "blossom-shaped cup" and a "platter, a dish"—are vessels used in each eucharistic celebration. The chalice is the most essential of all our liturgical vessels. The cup is prominent in the synoptic accounts of Christ instituting the eucharist and, in poetry and legend, the cup has been a strong image for Christians.

THE CHALICE EXPRESSES OUR THEOLOGY

Throughout the church's history we find the vessels, as expected, taking on the characteristics of each art period. But more interesting are the variations of size and shape in response to the theology of a given time. As long as there was participation of the faithful in the cup, it was large and generous, with a lip for drinking. When the priest alone was the recipient of the consecrated wine, the cup was reduced to almost egg-size while retaining a wide base, a high stem and an ornate knob.

Our treatment of the cup reflects our thinking about the church. Up to the Middle Ages, each church owned but one substantial chalice. What a strong symbol this was of these people, this church! In more recent times, the chalice has belonged to the priest.

VESSELS OF MANY MATERIALS

Cup and paten have been made of a variety of materials. We most often see gold, silver or glazed clay, but there have been cups of colored glass, bone, ivory, onyx, tin, pewter, crystal, stone, ebony (and other hard woods), and combinations of these.

Early Christians had vessels shaped like their drinking and eating vessels: beakers, cups, Roman-style bowls with two handles. What made them special was their use and the high esteem in which they were held—and their consequent decoration.

The scriptures establish the cup as a sign of extraordinary importance, the sign of the covenant in Jesus' blood, the sign of salvation. How then must we fashion and reverence this cup!

Excerpts from "The Cup of Salvation," by Regina Kuehn. Reprinted from *Liturgy 80*, May/June 1984, pp. 7–9.

---

not even be able to say, "Well, let's see. First, we said the Our Father. There's the peace greeting, then . . ."

If there is a way to view the whole communion rite, it would be something like this. When we have finished praising and thanking God over the bread and wine, become for us the body and blood of Christ, we pray the Lord's Prayer, embrace in the peace of Christ, then proceed to the breaking of the bread. Singing the Lamb of God litany and other songs, we come in procession together to eat a morsel of the holy bread and to drink a sip from the cup. We receive what we are, the body of Christ and the blood of Christ. Afterward, the whole assembly is quiet for some moments; then we pray that what we have done here may be reflected in every word and gesture of life.

Certainly the various parts of the rite need work and attention so that they can be habitually done well. This is not so that the participant will attend to or be impressed by the details of the rite. Rather, it frees the participant to be a part of what this parish is doing at such moments.

This is how the *General Instruction of the Roman Missal* (GIRM) describes the unity of the communion rite: "Since the eucharistic celebration is the paschal meal, in accord with his command, the body and blood of the Lord should be received as spiritual food by the faithful who are properly disposed. This is the purpose of the breaking of the bread and the other preparatory rites which lead directly to the communion of the people." (no. 56)

MINISTERS

The tasks and skills of the various ministers will become clear in the discussion of the rite. The ministers who are needed in the communion rite are: presider, cantor (or other leader of song in the absence of a cantor), ministers of communion, ushers. In addition, a deacon and one or more acolytes may have roles in this rite.

The overall presumption must be that those who minister do so as members of the assembly. Always remaining a part of the assembly, they perform some task in service to the assembly. That is the attitude all ministers are to have.

The presider, ordained and delegated by the bishop to preside for this assembly, is nevertheless first of all a baptized person who—like everyone else—joins this assembly because it is Sunday and on Sunday we celebrate the eucharist. At the communion rite, the presider's central task is to do that which was the first name Christians gave to their Sunday assemblies: the breaking of the bread. The presider also invites all to join in the Lord's Prayer (and leads the "Deliver us"), to exchange the peace greeting (unless a deacon is present to do this) and to come to the table. The presider will assist at the communion procession either with the bread or cup, will return to the chair for the silence and, from the chair, will speak the prayer after communion.

The cantor assists the assembly in the singing of the Lamb of God and the communion song. Usually the Lamb of God will be in a litany fashion: The cantor sings the first part and all respond with the unchanging (until the last time) "Have mercy on us." For the communion song, the cantor will usually sing the verses of a psalm or another song so that the assembly can sing a refrain or chorus that is unchanging. The cantor should understand what sort of music the communion rite requires and how it is best led: the Lamb of God, a mantra-like litany that fills the time for the breaking of the bread and leads directly into the invitation to the table; the communion song, allowing for much variety as long as its music and lyrics fit for a procession and for this particular procession. In the absence of a cantor, the organist or other instrumentalist usually becomes a leader of these songs.

Ministers of communion come forward from the assembly to assist with the breaking of the bread and pouring from the large cup or flagon into small cups; they take the bread and cups to the assembly and, after the procession, place the vessels on a side table and receive communion themselves. Their movements, gestures and words are marked by reverence and presence to the members of the assembly.

Ushers bring the peace greeting to any who might be isolated in the assembly and they bring good order to the communion procession.

Sometimes their presence is almost invisible. They are not traffic police but good hosts and hostesses—recognizing though that this is not their house but the house of the assembly.

The deacon is an assistant to the presider and the acolytes are assistants to the deacon (to the presider when there is no deacon). Between them they see to it that vessels and the sacramentary are in the proper places at the right times. They are to know the rite so well that they can attend to the expected details and the unexpected needs.

THE COMMUNION rite begins with a very simple invitation to pray as Jesus taught us to pray. Then together we speak the words of the Lord's Prayer. After the phrase "deliver us from evil," the presider continues alone in an elaboration of that phrase. This text brings us all back to acclaim: "For the kingdom, the power and the glory are yours, now and for ever."

The invitation comes first. Several things need attention in carrying out this moment in the rite:

▪ The invitation should be given only when the assembly is ready to hear it. If the assembly has been standing for the eucharistic prayer (a fitting posture for praise and thanksgiving), their Amen should be followed by a pause as the presider places cup and bread on the altar. If people have been kneeling, they need time to stand and attend. There is to be the sense of a transition from one intense moment in the ritual to one whose intensity is of quite a different order.

▪ The invitation should ordinarily be given with one of the four texts presented in the sacramentary. These are models of directness and brevity, not worn out after a few hearings. The invitation should be consistent over a number of Sundays of Ordinary Time or through all the Sundays of a season.

• The invitation is an invitation. It is spoken with directness to the assembly. This itself marks a change from the entire eucharistic prayer where the presider's words are addressed to God. The text, therefore, is spoken from memory, with eyes on the assembly and with hands joined.

• If the Lord's Prayer is to be sung, then the invitation should ordinarily be sung (to avoid some other musical cue coming between the invitation and the prayer).

• Once the invitation is given, the presider's voice should cease to dominate. People do not need to be led word by word. The presider should be just one voice among many (this is true for other recited texts as well).

All ministers, as part of their training, can learn to exercise well their role as the assembly; that is, they can be asked to do such things as speak up with the words "Our Father" when the invitation is given, thus relieving the presider of the feeling that no one is going to say anything.

SPOKEN OR SUNG

*I*f one element of the Lord's Prayer is sung, all should ordinarily be sung (invitation through acclamation), but sometimes a presider will not be able to sing the invitation or the "Deliver us."

In the Lord's Prayer, what matters is that everyone take part. The prayer should never be sung in ways that are not accessible to every member of the assembly. It is never a solo or a choir piece. It is not a litany or a time for verses and refrains. It should be sung by all throughout, straight through. A parish may be more comfortable with one melody than with another. There is no problem unless the melody is so elaborate that the words begin to be lost. The words will never be lost when the parish uses a chant (plainsong) melody. The presence of these melodies in the sacramentary should indicate that they are the norm. Be careful of departing too far from this.

Music for the Lord's Prayer serves to give us a common pace. It takes words that are already familiar, slows them down and lifts them up, bringing us all into one voice. Music written for specialists simply has no place here.

In recitation, there will always be some voices charging ahead and some bringing up the rear. That is always a problem with recitation. The majority will find their pace and keep it without a dominating voice coming through the public address system.

DELIVER US AND ACCLAMATION

*W*hen "Deliver us" is recited, the presider can help greatly by learning to use the voice in such a way that the last words ("for the coming of our Savior, Jesus Christ") will invite the acclamation ("For the kingdom . . ."). This is a matter of the rise and fall of the voice. It is not achieved through efforts at eye contact with the assembly (looking from one side to the other while speaking). After all, these words are not addressed to the assembly. It is a matter of attention and of inflection. Presiders can listen for what seems to work well. The acclamation should never seem like a detached piece. It is to flow right out of the presider's ". . . our Savior, Jesus Christ."

Presiders are discouraged from embellishing this text with brief homilies or thoughts. The whole text is itself an embellishment of the last lines of the Lord's Prayer. It does not need more. One author, asking why presiders are constantly changing "protect us from all anxiety" to "all undue anxiety" or something of the kind, points out that we should not fear the boldness of this text. Such is its confidence in God that we can ask for protection from *all* anxiety.

Music in the Communion Rite

It is sufficient introduction to say that the place of music in the communion rite is a more complicated question than whether or not to chant the Our Father, how to execute the Lamb of God or what song to sing for the distribution of the elements. The primary order of business for any liturgical musician is to understand how music serves the liturgical action.

The inherent litany structure of the Lamb of God should be respected. This is an eminently useful form for expanding the manifold meanings of a text that calls to mind the suffering servant imagery of Isaiah, the expiatory character of Christ's death, and the memorial of Jesus as the paschal lamb of the new covenant. To achieve such expansion, the *General Instruction of the Roman Missal* makes it quite clear that in this litany (which normally involves an interchange between cantor or choir and assembly) the invocations may be repeated as often as necessary to accompany the breaking of the bread (GIRM, 56). Thus the cantor intones any number of intercessions, each ending with the response "have mercy on us." The assembly joins in this plea.

During the procession, encourage congregational song without books or papers in hand. It is at least inconvenient to expect any congregation to carry hymnals during the procession. Select music with such a strong, simple refrain that it requires no textual aid. The cantor or choir can supplement with verses, leaving the assembly free to respond without the intrusion of books or pamphlets.

Select music that adequately supports the underlying liturgical movement, not only by its presence but also in mood and style. Considering the proces-

POSTURE

Everyone stands for the Lord's Prayer. In some places, they join hands. In other places, all take the posture of the presider (hands extended) or some modified version thereof. Note that:

▪ The sacramentary does not call for these gestures (but it would be quite out of character for it to specify such a gesture for the assembly).

▪ Such gestures should be introduced only if they will be done with complete consistency in all the parish Masses on every Sunday so that this becomes the way this parish prays the Lord's Prayer. No one should have to look around to see what to do. All attention should be free for the prayer itself.

▪ Because this is *the* common prayer of Christians, anything that introduces disunity should be avoided. In some places, it may be comfortable for one group to have hands joined and for other individuals to take a posture with arms extended and for the majority of the people just to stand and pray. Even when this is possible, it is not necessarily desirable.

---

sional nature of the ritual, ministerial integrity calls for the use of music best described as acclamatory. Though acclamatory is not necessarily equivalent to loud, the selection should speak a vitality and rhythm that reflects an attitude of proclamation, affirmation of faith in the significance of this action (as Paul suggests in 1 Corinthians 11:26).

Music should accompany the entire procession, from the invitation to communion to the time of silence before the prayer after communion. This presumes songs that are adequate in length. One song for the entire activity is best, thus modeling unity. This might require interludes, improvisations, *ad libitum* choral renderings and other alternatives during the course of the song. These are valuable in breaking the monotony of an unvaried interchange between cantor and congregation. If the song runs out, do not arbitrarily add another. This usually is musically disruptive, calling forth possible changes of key, meter, text, thought and page. It gives the impression that the primary value is to "keep the music coming," an impression also made by repeating verses already sung. It is far better to continue instrumentally in the same mode: improvising on the hymn, changing registration, dividing melody and harmony between manuals or allowing various instruments to carry the melody at a changed dynamic level.

Excerpts from "Planning the Music," by Edward Foley. Reprinted from *It Is Your Own Mystery*, pp. 35–37. Copyright © 1977, The Liturgical Conference, Washington, D.C. All rights reserved. Used with permission.

Together they resound the most basic words the follower of Jesus has to say.

▪ When one or the other posture is adopted by the parish, it need not be asked for. It is simply to be done without invitation from the presider.

▪ If joining hands or extending hands are to be general practice, then all those ministers (acolytes, lectors) in the sightlines of the assembly should take part and should do so with grace and seriousness. This is true also of those ministers (the ushers especially) who are seen by only a few but whose example is extremely important. The ushers, in fact, may be the very ones to invite for discussion before any gestures are introduced for the assembly.

▪ Such gestures would conclude when the acclamation concludes. Again, the presider and other visible ministers need to give example.

All in all, it may be best to take the rubrics literally: The presider is to have hands extended for the Lord's Prayer and the "Deliver us," and then hands folded for the acclamation. The assembly has no uniform posture.

SAY THIS WHEN YOU PRAY

The Lord's Prayer stands at the opening moment of the communion rite. It is a crucial part of the Christian's vocabulary. The words of this prayer are the words of our scriptures, not only of the gospel story when the disciples ask Jesus to teach them to pray, but of the whole tradition that Jesus drew on when he prayed. The words are from the depths of the Hebrew Scriptures. Within the Christian churches, they have been the summation of all our prayer, the text that was given to the catechumens only after they had been chosen for the Easter sacraments. The *Rite of Christian Initiation of Adults* says: "From antiquity the Lord's Prayer has been the prayer proper to those who in baptism have received the spirit of adoption." (no. 149) This is the prayer that Christians once recited several times every day, especially on waking and retiring. This remains a firm practice of many Christians, young and old.

The Lord's Prayer in the Mass is one bond between the Christian's daily prayer and the prayer of the assembly. One echoes the other as they together resound the most basic words the follower of Jesus has to say. One would wish that these words would find their way occasionally into the Sunday homily (which, according to GIRM, no. 41, is to take the liturgical texts as well as the scriptures as its foundation). We need to be called on to reflect about what it is to say "hallowed be thy name" or "give us this day our daily bread" or "deliver us from evil."

If the Lord's Prayer is to be like a chant binding our days and years together, binding us likewise to one another, then some mystagogical preaching is in order now and again: something that will unfold these words one more time for our new hearing and speaking. Such preaching could also embrace the extended text of the "Deliver us": This is one of the church's stark recognitions of the evil with which we struggle. In this struggle we pray without shame for God's deliverance.

THE PRESIDER has hands joined for the acclamation that concludes the Lord's Prayer. A change in posture requires a needed moment of transition to the sign of peace. The rubric before the prayer "Lord Jesus Christ" says, "The priest, with hands extended, says aloud . . ." With this change in posture comes a change of pace. The communal engagement in the Lord's Prayer has ended and now comes a rather low-key prayer spoken by the presider. The rite is harmed by efforts to make every moment intense. This prayer should be quiet and unembellished. Expansions of this text— impromptu or rehearsed—dilute its simple intercessions. This prayer is not a major moment, just a transition.

The directives of the sacramentary make it clear that the sign of peace is both important and optional:

> Before they share in the same bread, the people express their love for one another and beg for peace and unity in the church and with all humankind. The form of this rite is left to the conference of bishops to decide in accord with the customs and mentality of the people. (GIRM, no. 56)

The words "The peace of the Lord be with you always" are a fixed part of the liturgy, but the following rubric makes the invitation optional: "Then the deacon (or the priest) may add: Let us offer each other the sign of peace. All make an appropriate sign of peace, according to local custom.

The priest gives the sign of peace to the deacon or minister." The optional nature of this sign of peace is stressed here only because there may be occasions when it is best to exercise that option. Examples would include some Masses with children or Masses when, for one reason or another, a

Augustine: What We Learn at This Table

This is surely what we read in the Proverbs of Solomon: "If you sit down to eat at the table of a ruler, observe carefully what is set before you; then stretch out your hand, knowing that you must provide the same kind of meal yourself." What is this ruler's table if not the one at which we receive the body and blood of him who laid down his life for us? What does it mean to sit at this table if not to approach it with humility? What does it mean to stretch out one's hand, knowing that one must provide the same kind of meal oneself, if not what I have just said: As Christ laid down his life for us, so we in our turn ought to lay down our lives for our brothers and sisters. This is what the apostle Paul said: "Christ suffered for us, leaving us an example, that we might follow in his footsteps."

This is what is meant by providing "the same kind of meal." This is what the blessed martyrs did with such burning love. If we are to give true meaning to our celebration of their memorials, to our approaching the Lord's table in the very banquet at which they were fed, we must, like them, provide "the same kind of meal."

At this table of the Lord we do not commemorate the martyrs in the same way as we commemorate others who rest in peace. We do not pray for the martyrs as we pray for those others; rather, they pray for us, that we may follow in their footsteps. They practiced the perfect love of which the Lord said

there could be none greater. They provided "the same kind of meal" as they had themselves received at the Lord's table.

This must not be understood as saying that we can be the Lord's equals by bearing witness to him to the extent of shedding our blood. He had the power of laying down his life; we by contrast cannot choose the length of our lives, and we die even if it is against our will. He, by dying, destroyed death in himself; we are freed from death only in his death. His body did not see corruption; our body will see corruption and only then be clothed through him in incorruption at the end of the world. He needed no help from us in saving us; without him we can do nothing. He gave himself to us as the vine to the branches; apart from him we cannot have life.

Finally, even if one dies for another, yet no martyr by shedding blood brings forgiveness for the sins of others, as Christ brought forgiveness to us. In this he gave us, not an example to imitate but a reason for rejoicing. Inasmuch, then, as they shed their blood for others, the martyrs provided "the same kind of meal" as they had received at the Lord's table. Let us then love one another as Christ loved us and gave himself up for us.

All ministers join in the sign of peace, acolytes and ushers and musicians as well as presider and deacon and lectors.

sign of peace is appropriate at another time within the liturgy and need not be duplicated here. Such occasions will be rare. The norm at Sunday liturgy is the sign of peace.

PARTICULARS

*P*arish practice might take the following into account when working with the peace greeting:

▪ The deacon or presider, in inviting the assembly to offer a sign of peace, should beware of wordy invitations. Too often this becomes an opportunity to get three or four quick sentences that harken back to the

Where Everybody Shares Alike

Consider that sacramental act, the holy meal. This is the entire symbolic action in which the good news of our new life in the reign of God through our common baptismal death is proclaimed by rite, by gesture, by sign, by movement, by touch, by the honor and reverence given to all, by our eating and drinking commonly together. Just as the word is proclaimed and preached to all who will listen, without regard to station or status, so the baptismal death that accepts the new dominion and life of the reign of God, the kingdom, is offered to all on the sole condition of conversion. The banquet of the reign of God to which that baptismal death admits us is therefore no longer a domestic feast—not even one with an empty seat for the outsider and the reject. It is now an ecclesial feat, utterly common, free of distinction of sex, color, class, nation, property, power, even of family.

This is not an ideology, but it is certainly an experience, a human experience, that should have profound social consequences. It is not an ideology, not a blueprint for society, because it has to serve succeeding systems of social organization—and in much the same way. The banquet of the kingdom enables believers in all of those succeeding systems to be free of every system's claims to absolutism by acknowledgment of the sole dominion of the God of history and by the celebration of our true destiny, a destiny of freedom and oneness (not a choice between them and never a preference of the demands of one over the other).

The sacrament is the parable or story in action. It is no accident that parable and sacrament are the common ways in which people of biblical faith renew and express and share their identity as church, as covenant people. Jesus would rather paint a picture in words, tell a story, let us think about a story, let us figure out how we fit into that picture and what it means for our lives. It is a way of communicating that is neither nondirective nor dictatorial, but very conscious of the mystery of our decisions, our differences, our variety, very reverent and respectful toward the hearer.

When we celebrate the eucharist we play kingdom. The liturgy places us in a new situation, the reign of God, and it opens a new kind of existence where we are simply daughters and sons of God, all sinners, all loved and graced, with none of the world's distinctions and roles and castes and sexes and classes and colors. Because liturgy is a human and social enterprise, we have to have different roles, a variety of specialized ministries, beginning with the ministry of the entire assembly, with different people doing different things to contribute to the common celebration. But the roles and the different parts we play are strictly services to the whole community, within the limits of the basic egalitarianism of baptismal initiation—totally distinct from the categories of society and power and money.

Where else in our society are all of us—not just a gnostic elite, but everyone—called to be social critics, called to extricate ourselves from the powers and principalities that claim to rule our daily lives, in order to submit ourselves to the sole dominion of the God before whom all of us are equal? Where else in our society are we all addressed and sprinkled and

homily. Resist the urge. The invitation could be varied as long as it is as brief and direct as the wording given in the sacramentary. What is to be avoided is offering reasons or motivations or descriptions. Just invite. The assembly knows the rhythm here. People are not listening for a message, just a go-ahead.

▪ All ministers who are positioned where they can be seen by the assembly must join in the sign of peace. This means acolytes and ushers and musicians as well as presider and deacon and lectors. This is preparation to exercise any of these ministries. It means that one does not cease to be a member of the assembly by becoming an acolyte or an usher.

bowed to and incensed and touched and kissed and treated like *somebody*—all in the very same way? Where else do economic czars and beggars get the same treatment? Where else are food and drink blessed in a common prayer of thanksgiving, broken and poured out, so that everybody, everybody shares and shares alike?

We are beginning to realize the social consequences of a eucharistic liturgy celebrated not merely as an obligation, not merely as an unreformed society at prayer, not merely as the pious face of an otherwise troubled world, but now as an expression of God's marvelous and continuing deeds for the transformation of human life and human society. We can see already that these beginnings are leading us into uncharted ways—to a social conscience and a social mission that goes far beyond individual and private compassion to a corporate responsibility for changing structures and systems. We can feel already the fear and withdrawal and reaction of great parts and elements of the church—a church still far too much a cultural phenomenon and not yet a conscious community of initiated converts.

We experience these beginnings in a world that seems to be on every level retreating from whatever promise its structures have exhibited of understanding that the poor and the hungry can no longer be hidden. Now that it has become clear to us how radical a change our emerging social consciousness requires, reaction and retreat is as natural as sin.

Yet we believe. We have died with Christ in baptism. We celebrate the mystery of life through death at every Sunday assembly. We are prepared for struggle, for disappointment, for apparent failure even, because we are not responsible for the fulfillment of the reign of God, for the full realization of the liberation and the unification of humanity in God. We are responsible only for today, only for living this moment with the kind of vision that Mass nourishes, the kind of love that Mass feeds, the kind of struggle against the status quo that Mass signifies. Our commitment is not to results. It is to the life we live today, and to making it count.

Excerpts from "The Mass and Its Social Consequences," by Robert W. Hovda. Reprinted from *Liturgy 80*, June/July 1982, pp. 2–6.

▪ To whom should the ministers go? That depends on the arrangement of the room and their place within it. If possible, they should be close enough to the other members of the assembly that the peace greeting can be exchanged back and forth. The presider and deacon are not to spend a large amount of time "working the crowd" (because, for all the good intentions, that is what it most often resembles), but they should go beyond greeting other ministers. The presider needs a sense of the assembly: By the time the people are finished with the greeting, the presider should be back at the altar. Ushers have a special responsibility during the peace greeting. They can make sure that those who are sitting

History of the Peace Greeting

The gesture designated as the kiss of peace is already present in the early accounts of the Roman eucharistic liturgy written by Justin Martyr in the second century and by Hippolytus in the third. St. Paul, too, had enjoined the Romans and Corinthians to greet one another with "a holy kiss" (Romans 16:16; 1 Corinthians 16:20), although it is not clear that Paul's exhortation refers to a liturgical context. The testimony of art and letters together shows that the pax has covered a whole range of stylized gestures of embrace in the course of liturgical history. Beneath the range of variant gestures, however, a religious intent has been constant.

In the earliest eucharistic liturgies, the pax consistently appeared at the close of the word service, "as a seal," they said, of what had taken place. But what had taken place? The living word proclaimed in the midst of the assembly had purified them and renewed them in the Holy Spirit of Jesus. The mutual embrace was a gesture of acknowledging and confirming the holienss of the ecclesial body of Christ, now ready to make eucharist with the risen Lord. Implicit or explicit in the exchange was the intent to reconcile any differences among members of the body and to bring them into communion with one another.

Only later did the Roman church move the pax to a position after the completion of the eucharistic prayer, still as the "seal" of all that had taken place. But it seems that in St. Augustine's church in North Africa the aspect of reconciliation had gained prominence. As a result, by the sixth century, the Western church was explaining the pax not so much as a seal of what had already occurred but rather as a dramatic enactment of the phrase from the Lord's prayer, "Forgive us as we forgive . . ." Thus mutual forgiveness, reconciliation and communion in the one Spirit in the one body had a single expression in the gesture of peace. So real and long-standing was this understanding of the pax as profound communion that one medieval religious community called for the spiritual communion of the pax as the cul-

alone are greeted with peace. When possible, they can reach out to those who are visitors. Ministers of communion will usually be using this opportunity to give the peace greeting to persons along the aisles as these ministers make their way to the area around the altar.

▪ Should there be singing or instrumental music during the greeting? Normally, no. Those who would make such music should, at this time, be taken up in the sign of peace. They are members of the assembly and that should show. An organist should leave the organ bench. Background music is almost always inappropriate—except in those parishes where

---

mination of its daily eucharist, reserving communion with the sacramental elements to Sundays.

A serious shift and distortion of Christian religious consciousness in the medieval period left its impact on the gesture of peace in the eucharistic liturgy. As it came to be thought that the Spirit of the risen Lord resided in power only in the consecrated elements and in the ordained clergy but not in the merely baptized, the laity were omitted from the gesture. That development engendered a further weakening of faith and a diminishment in appreciation of the mystery of the Lord's presence. The gesture of peace extended through the assembly had expressed confidence that the Spirit of the Lord was already present in all the baptized. Elimination of the gesture served to minimize the importance of the assembly.

Can the primitive faith pattern be recovered? Ritual touch is itself occasion for some awkwardness among 20th century Americans. Ritual touch which expressed conviction that the two persons reaching out to one another are filled with the Holy Spirit and acknowledge this mystery in one another is more than awkward. It calls for great faith. It demands that we first overcome the great doubt we

have about ourselves, and then that we overcome our doubts about others, either because we know them or because we don't. How much easier it is to limit belief in the Lord's presence to the consecrated bread and wine on the altar table and to the priest who handles them!

Genuine spiritual renewal of the church and the church's liturgy will come in proportion to the confidence with which the whole adult community can reach out to touch each other with a confident and hopeful greeting of peace. What more direct way to confess: We do believe in the mystery of incarnation and the mystery of resurrection as the way to salvation. If the church assembled on Sunday is not confident of itself as a Spirit-filled community, the body of Christ, further liturgical action is without foundation and to no purpose. Extending the gesture of peace in anticipation of eucharistic communion is simultaneously an expression of faith and an antidote to unbelief.

Excerpts from "Historical Perspectives," by Mary Collins. Reprinted from *It Is Your Own Mystery*, pp. 8–13. Copyright © 1977, The Liturgical Conference, Washington, D.C. All rights reserved. Used with permission.

*It is a time to manifest
as best we can the peace
that Jesus prayed for
and that we pray for.*

the peace greeting lasts a long time. In some communities, this lengthy exchange has become the steady practice. One could say that it is not what is expected by the rite, but people would answer that it does indeed indicate and create peace and prepare for communion. It is certainly preferable to the perfunctory murmur that is all some parishes can manage. Still, in those parishes where the peace greeting tends to run on and on, some music after a few minutes may serve to draw the assembly back to a common focus on the altar. This music can be the prelude to the Lamb of God.

▪ What controls the length of this greeting is the furniture. It is not a time for socializing, exchanging words about health or weather, or even for exchanging holiday greetings. It is a time to manifest as best we can the peace that Jesus prayed for and that we pray for. Within the limits allowed by the furniture, then, the greeting with handshake or embrace should be extended by each to many others. Not everyone need go into the aisles, but those sitting alongside the aisle should always feel that it is acceptable to cross the aisle or move up and down the aisle. The manner of the ushers and communion ministers will help set a tone.

As with the Lord's Prayer, so with the sign of peace, there would be occasions for the homilist to speak on this rite. This should get quite specific about the rite and what we need to give to it. The Easter season especially offers opportunities for exploring both the meaning of this rite and the manner in which it is done within the parish. This is the time of mystagogia when the sacramental mysteries are unfolded for the newly baptized and for all of us. Surely among the mysteries that need reflection each year are those we celebrate with our words and songs and gestures of the eucharist.

THE BREAKING OF THE BREAD

N THE SIGN of peace every member of the assembly becomes aware that this is an assembly of many different individuals: different faces, sexes, ages, backgrounds. As soon as the focus returns to the altar, the presider lifts up the bread and breaks it. In this gesture, the church since apostolic times has seen its own mystery. The "breaking of the bread" was the name they first gave their gatherings.

The gesture stands without words from the presider. The only words belong to the assembly and the cantor as the Lamb of God is sung. The breaking of the bread is described in the sacramentary in this way:

> In addition to its practical aspect, it signifies that in communion we who are many are made one body in the one bread of life which is Christ (see 1 Corinthians 10:17). (GIRM, no. 56)

It has this "practical aspect" first, one that we often neglect, preferring to take care of all practicalities privately. But, as usual, we can't have one without the other. Without the practical aspect, real bread to be really broken, there is hardly a chance that we will grasp any deeper significance. Since the Roman Missal was revised in 1969, it has contained this direction:

> The eucharistic bread, even though unleavened and traditional in form, should therefore be made in such a way that the priest can break

it and distribute the parts to at least some of the faithful. . . . The gesture of the breaking of the bread, as the eucharist was called in apostolic times, will more clearly show the eucharist as a sign of unity and charity, since the one bread is being distributed among the members of one family. (GIRM, no. 283)

This stands at the head of any discussion about the breaking of the bread: The presider takes the large loaf of bread, raises it above the plate in the sight of all and breaks it in two and then into pieces. The assembly sings the Lamb of God while this is done. Whatever is done about the cup, whether there are communion ministers or not, this initial breaking and the beginning of the singing are to be done with such attention and reverence (and without competing sights and sounds) that we, like our ancestors, would have the good sense to call this whole gathering "the breaking of the bread." That is how clear it should be that in this moment we have summed up the meaning of our assembly, our church. Even

The Cup: Every Sunday, Every Mass

When introducing the regular practice of communion from the cup, first thought is always given to preparing the community at large, but they are far from the only ones. Begin with the parish staff, then the ministers of the eucharist, other ministers and finally the community.

PREPARING THE STAFF

Regard "staff" in the broadest sense: school faculty, CCD catechists, parish council, liturgy team, leaders of parish societies, the clergy and other pastoral associates. Count as important anyone in a position to influence attitudes and receptivity of the parish or who will be meeting with significant groups of parishioners—from the Holy Name Society to the parents of first communicants. Before communion from the cup is initiated all such persons may well benefit from a time of reflection and discussion together on this practice.

Nothing will be so detrimental as an attitude on the part of any staff, especially the clergy, which indicates that communion from the cup is unnecessary, too time consuming, superfluous or costly. We have taught ourselves so well for so long that Christ is present fully under either species that it is certainly possible that some will not appreciate the importance of the full sharing in the eucharistic meal. Insuring that the core parish staff and extended staff value extending communion from the cup each Sunday will go a long way toward removing any obstacles to this practice. Take time to identify and reflect together on issues of Christ's presence in the eucharist, the fullness of sign in communion from the cup, the history which only gradually removed the cup from the faithful, the gradual restoration of the cup to the community since Vatican II.

A most helpful resource is "From Human Meal to Christian Eucharist" by Philippe Rouillard which originally appeared in English in *Worship* (September 1978 and January 1979 and reprinted in *Living Bread, Saving Cup,* published by The Liturgical Press in 1982). Rouillard's discussion—of hunger, nourishment, life, the symbolism of bread and wine, the sacred meals in the Hebrew Scriptures, the meals of Christ in the gospel and the evolution of the eucharistic meal in the church—is superbly readable and insightful background.

PREPARING THE MINISTERS OF COMMUNION

For both new and veteran ministers of communion it is imperative to walk through the communion rite on site before implementation day. This "getting my part straight" is a *sine qua non.* Equally important is time for the ministers to consider the meaning of their service to the community. The section "Touchstones for Ministers of Communion" on page 38 presents the essence of this ministry and gives parish leaders a sense of whom to invite to this ministry.

We Roman Catholics have learned by our practice (despite our teaching about the presence of Christ in both species) that the cup is not essential. The parish needs a policy of rotating the responsibilities when there are numerous ministers of communion and plates and cups to be brought forward, all should wait on this first gesture and the beginning of the litany.

In this discussion of the breaking of the bread, much practical information, covering everything from a bread recipe to sample bulletin inserts on communion from the cup, is to be found in the supplementary materials.

WHAT THE BREAKING OF THE BREAD SHOULD LOOK LIKE

The communion ministers come forward during the peace greeting and take places near the altar (but not between the assembly and the presider). Like the rest of the assembly, their attention is then on the presider. If, by the time the ministers reach the area around the altar, the peace greeting has ended, they refrain from greeting one another. Otherwise, from the assembly's angle, this looks too much like friends just running into one another and shaking hands. The exchange of the peace greeting among the ministers should happen only if the peace is still being exchanged in the assembly.

among all the ministers to the cup and of having the presider and any assisting priests regularly take a turn ministering the cup.

A minimum of two gatherings for training is necessary in a parish of some size. One evening of reflection on the eucharist, on our experience of communion and on the nature and parts of the communion rite is a good background appreciated by the ministers. It is too easy to let this role be purely functional. For those parishes which have not instituted regular in-service training and formation for liturgical ministers, this can be an occasion to announce an expectation of their participation in periodic gatherings for such formation.

A second session is required for walking through and rehearsing the rite and for matters of scheduling. Offering each session more than once will be very successful if too many people are involved to expect perfect attendance at a once-only meeting.

A walk-through should be precise and well planned. At the theological reflection session, each minister can receive a written description of how the communion rite will look. Now, at one location, experienced communion ministers train small groups of ministers in the basics of ministering the bread and the cup. A second area shows procedures after Mass: at the credence table, tabernacle and sacristy. The basics here are caring for the vessels, how to use the purificators, where they were kept, handling the vessels after communion, cleaning vessels after Mass. The last and most obviously needed of the learning areas is for going through the

The presider takes the bread and waits for the cantor (or organist or other instrumentalist) to begin the Lamb of God. As this begins, the presider breaks the bread. It is a substantial piece of bread that is broken, so substantial that the word "loaf" (as used previously) is entirely appropriate.

With the rest of the assembly, the communion ministers join in the beginning responses to the Lamb of God. See the notes on the Lamb of God in the discussion of music for the communion rite on page 17. There are two important things to note:

communion rite itself. This includes every moment from coming from their places in the assembly, to where they are to stand, to how to assist with breaking of the bread, and so on through to returning to their places. Allow people time to surface their questions about procedure.

A new ministry is often needed when attendance is large. It can be called the service minister. This person is entrusted with refilling the cups as necessary during the reception of communion, seeing to any other needs of the communion ministers and dealing with accidents. At the end of communion, this minister can be at the side table to receive the vessels from the communion ministers and to cover vessels with a cloth until they are cleaned after Mass. Perhaps this minister would also assist with clearing the table and cleaning before the next Mass. An experienced minister of communion is needed for this position.

PREPARING THE OTHER MINISTERS

Other ministers need to be on board before implementation day, especially the sacristans, the ushers and the musicians. If you have no sacristans on duty during the Sunday Masses, you will need them now.

The care, storage, preparation and cleaning of vessels is no small task. It is not for the presider or young acolytes to be concerned with preparation of bread, wine, linens and vessels between Masses.

A key job of the sacristan will be estimating how much bread and wine to have prepared for each liturgy. For several Sundays before implementation day, do a count of communicants at each Mass to get a sense of how much variance there is from week to week and to learn the average number of communicants. After beginning communion from the cup, the sacristan is to keep precise records of how much bread and wine is set out for each Mass. A month's experience is enough to judge the proper amount. A sacristan who regularly serves each Mass will quickly learn to adjust that amount for the numbers present.

The ushers, an often overlooked group, need and deserve to know what is going on. Where ushers have not been used to assist the community in *procession* to communion, this is a grand opportunity to enlist their support and to begin an ordered communion procession. The placement of communion stations is to be adjusted to introduce communion from the cup and the ushers are the best of resources to aid the transition.

- This is a litany. That is a form of prayer in which the assembly needs no text or music. Their part is to repeat a refrain over and over against the invocations sung by a cantor or choir. A litany is quite different from a hymn or an acclamation. It thrives on the play of repetition by all against variety by the leader. It is very difficult to have a recited litany. Litanies call out for some sort of chanting, where the words and music fit together in patterns that set us free to pray with the images of the invocations.

- The sacramentary notes: "This invocation may be repeated as often as necessary to accompany the breaking of the bread, and is brought to a

---

The musicians need "troped" settings of the Lamb of God and they need to know when to begin and end this litany. Your musicians will appreciate being invited to the rehearsal of communion ministers to get a clearer idea of the shape of the communion rite and when any music can begin and end.

Remember as well to inform by spoken word, by letter, by diagram   in every possible way—all the other ministers of when and how they themselves are to receive communion.

PREPARING THE PARISH COMMUNITY

It is my experience that parishioners are more likely to say, "At last!" than "What now!" to the announcement of communion from the cup on Sunday. Their best preparation has been gradual introduction to the practice on other occasions, especially the great days like Holy Thursday, Easter Vigil and Corpus Christi at which a large assembly would have received communion from the cup.

Preparing the community for the cup can be a fine occasion to broaden appreciation of the symbolism of bread and wine (see the Rouillard article mentioned previously), to refresh a sense of history for how, in the beginning and for nearly 13 centuries, it was the right of the faithful to receive from the cup: see Josef Jungmann, *Mass of the Roman Rite* and Mary Collins in *It Is Your Own Mystery* [ed. Melissa Kay, The Liturgical Conference, 1977]. Discuss the whole of the communion rite and not only the procedure for drinking from the cup.

Bulletin articles, homilies, extended communion announcements are all fine means of spreading the word. The more means we use, the better the chance of reaching people. The Easter season is a good time for this preparation since the season itself reflects on our experience of the initiation sacraments, especially the eucharist. This is the time of mystagogia, as the catechumenate calls it, time to relish our experience of the sacred mysteries. But the most effective long-term catechesis on the communion rite will be the actual experience of that rite if it is graciously and simply executed. Immediate preparation of the community will certainly include a demonstration of how to receive and drink from the cup, what to say, where to stand, and how the minister will wipe and turn the cup.

Excerpts from "The Cup: Every Sunday, Every Mass," by Mary Ann Simcoe. Reprinted from *Liturgy 80*, May/June 1985, pp. 5–8.

*Until now, only one plate,
one cup and one larger
container of wine have been
on the altar.*

close by the words, grant us peace." (GIRM, no. 56) Contrary to what is
still typical practice, the Lamb of God is not a set of three units. It is a
litany that accompanies the breaking of the bread. Where there is sadly
no real breaking of the bread and all is ready in a matter of seconds, the
Lamb of God has no function in the liturgy at all. But where a true
breaking takes place and where there are cups to be filled from the large
vessel, then the chanting should continue as long as the action. The
leader (cantor or organist or other instrumentalist) needs to attend to
what is taking place at the altar. When the presider is standing still before
the plate and cup, then the litany may be concluded with its final "grant
us peace."

After the presider has begun to break the bread, designated
ministers bring the needed plates and cups to the altar. Until now, only
one plate, one cup and one larger container of wine have been on the altar.
Usually one minister brings the cups, using a tray if more than two are
needed. The cup on the altar, the one used by the presider, will always be
one of the cups used for the communion of the assembly. A second
minister brings the plates for the eucharistic bread. The ministers may

take these trays with their vessels from the side table (credence table) when they come forward during the peace greeting, but they should stand in place holding the vessels until the breaking of the bread has begun. When they then come forward with the vessels, these two ministers begin to assist the presider: One helps to break and distribute the bread, the other takes the large container of wine and begins to fill the smaller cups. If all of the bread is in large pieces, more than one minister should come forward to assist in the breaking. The presider, in this case, is to break the large pieces at least once and then is to place the large but once-broken pieces in one of the smaller plates, giving this to an assisting minister.

The breaking and pouring should be visible to the assembly. Ministers should stand so that they do not obstruct this. The tasks of

Why Share the Cup?

The eucharistic celebration never ended with the eucharistic prayer, nor with the breaking of the bread. There has always been eating and drinking, even when done only by the priest celebrant. The crucial human action was preserved, but this action was often barely recognizable.

We often take for granted the fact that it is wine that is placed on our altar, to be consecrated and to be shared. Wine—something that already has significance in most homes and communities. Jesus did not select wine as one among many choices, as if any liquid could have carried his meaning. As bread is the staff of life, so wine is life's delight. Its presence means and brings festivity and rejoicing. Yet it also holds within itself meanings of death and of acceptance and of covenant. In the long tradition which Jesus shared, wine was for the praise of God whose creation delighted the heart. Jesus raised the cup and pronounced the blessings throughout his life: "Blessed are you, Lord God of all creation, for you have given us the fruit of the vine."

The *bread*, the body of Christ, does not cease to mean the nourishing fruit of the earth and the good-tasting work of human hands when we take it in holy communion. The *wine*, the blood of Christ, does not cease to mean delight, festivity and communion with each other. Christ's body and blood are bound up in creation, in fruitfulness, in human work, in communal rejoicing, in redemption. Wine nourishes our thirsty spirits. It is spiritual drink. By taking the cup, we express the deepest fellowship with the Lord Jesus even in the sharing of his death. Such diverse things—the delight of fellowship, the communion in his death! The cup, shared among us, brings these together.

breaking and pouring are gestures to be practiced. Too often they seem almost furtive, hurried. They should be done with reverence and care and a fullness that is shown by lifting up the cup that is being filled or by holding the bread being broken above the plate.

Note that no one goes to the tabernacle to bring eucharistic bread from another liturgy. (For more on this, scc page 43 and the supplementary material on page 76.)

Touchstones for Ministers of Communion

1. You have been called to a most beautiful ministry. Time taken to reflect on its meaning and practice will deeply enrich your own awareness of the mystery of Christ and that of the people you serve.

2. The communion rite is the ritual climax of the entire eucharistic liturgy. The gathering of the community, the proclamation of God's word, the remembering and thanksgiving and offering in the eucharistic prayer—all are directed toward the moment of communion in which we many, fed with his own body and blood, are made one in the Lord.

3. "Would you understand the body of Christ? Hear the Apostle saying to the faithful: 'You are the body and members of Christ.' If, then, you are Christ's body and his members, it is your own mystery which you receive. It is to what you are that you reply 'Amen,' and by replying subscribe. For you are told, 'The body of Christ,' and you reply, 'Amen.' Be a member of the body of Christ and let your 'Amen' be true." —St. Augustine

4. A primary qualification for ministers of communion, then, in light of the above, is that they be by nature interested in, caring about, at ease with other people—without regard for status in the community or for distinctions of class, sex, age or race. *All* who gather at the table of the Lord do so as sisters and brothers in the Lord and must be welcomed there as such.

5. An important principle for ministers of communion is *do not rush*. Allow this moment its full ritual beauty.

6. This is *not* a ministry for efficiency experts, nor for those who are unable to look another in the eye with comfort or to touch another person with ease. Nothing is more important in this ministry than the ability to focus your attention on the person to whom you are ministering. The meeting of minister and communicant is only for a moment. If you are looking down the approaching line or scanning the congregation instead of giving full attention to the person before you, something important will be lost. You must be able to disregard everything and everyone else in that moment, to look at the person before you with undivided attention. The look should be one of warmth and friendliness. You are greeting a brother or sister in Christ.

The communion ministers not needed at the altar wait in their places near the table. One by one, as plates and cups are filled, they approach and receive a vessel (and a purificator). The one who has taken the vessel then goes immediately to the place where he or she will serve the assembly. Thus, all the time that the Lamb of God is being sung and the bread is being broken, the number of ministers at the table is diminishing and the number at their stations is growing. Finally, the two

7. The communion into which Jesus invites us is a personal communion, a communion of persons. It is your ministry to make the moment of communion as personal as possible.

8. Speak to that person—not to the air or to the bread or to the cup. Hold up the bread or the cup and, looking the person in the eye, say, "The body of Christ," "The blood of Christ." Wait for the response: "Amen."

9. Gently place the bread in the outstretched palm or on the tongue of the person—allowing each the opportunity to indicate the manner of receiving. When placing the bread in a person's hand, be firm and do not rush. Let your hand touch the hand of the communicant. Hand the cup to the communicant, allowing your hands to touch. When the cup is returned, carefully wipe the rim with the purificator; then raise your eyes to welcome the next communicant.

10. *All* attention should be focused on the act of moving and singing together, eating together, experiencing our communion in and with the Lord.

11. Your reverence for the persons you serve and for the sacrament will show itself in all your actions:

a. In the way you walk (slowly, with dignity) as you approach the altar, usually during the breaking of the bread. Customs vary. You may be asked to bring extra plates or cups to the altar at this time, to assist the presider in breaking the bread or in filling cups. Or you may simply stand to the side or rear of the altar until handed a plate or cup. Whatever you do, do it with care and attention.

b. In the way you stand when you take your position at a communion station—with good posture, but relaxed, without stiffness. This is not a business transaction, remember, but a family meal, an act of personal communion.

c. In the way you hold the plate—carefully with one hand while ministering with the other.

d. In the way you hold the cup—with one hand, using the other to hold the cloth with which you wipe the rim after each communicant has received.

e. In the way you minister—with unhurried, deliberate movements.

12. You who serve in the ministry of communion are exercising the role of hosts and servants at the eucharistic banquet.

who have been assisting complete their tasks, take plate or cup and go to their stations. Except when a deacon is present, one minister will remain with the presider. After the presider's communion, this minister and the presider take the large plate and the main chalice and go to their communion stations. If there is a deacon, then both presider and deacon remain at the table; one will take the large plate and the other will take the chalice for the distribution of communion.

During the breaking of the bread the presider does the "commingling," dropping a small piece of the bread into the cup. The presider also says quietly one of the prayers that begins "Lord Jesus Christ." "Quietly," in the rubrics, means inaudibly. (But note that these two prayers can be part of the eucharistic catechesis of every child and adult and that they could be learned as silent prayers at communion time.)

At their stations, the ministers would turn back toward the presider, though in some cases it may be better for them to remain facing the assembly, holding plate or cup in readiness.

This approach to the ritual has the ministers receiving communion after the assembly. This is in accord with the rubrics, but is not as yet the common practice. Most parishes still place the communion ministers first. This usually means a lengthy pause between the invitation to communion ("This is the Lamb of God . . .") and the actual communion procession. Allowing the ministers to go directly to their stations and to receive communion after the other members of the

God's Invitation to Eat _and_ Drink

If we think of communion merely as a divinely ordained way of receiving Christ, then we will be satisfied to receive him under the species of bread alone, for having received him thus we cannot receive any more. If, however, we think of communion as our response to God's invitation to go to the Lord's table and to partake with joy of that banquet which celebrates the new covenant of Christ's sacrificed, self-giving love, then we will want not only to eat but to drink as well. This in essence is the significance of communion under both kinds.

—Harold Winston

assembly does two things: It makes for an orderly movement through the communion rite and it presents these ministers precisely as ministers.

Even if the ministers do not go to their stations before the words of invitation, they should receive their vessels and stand behind the presider, then go directly to their stations after the response, "Lord, I am not worthy . . ." They receive communion after the rest of the assembly.

BREAD

The principles about the bread are three.

1. *The bread is to appear to the senses as food.* We are quite simply to recognize bread. This is spelled out in the *General Instruction of the Roman Missal:*

> The nature of the sign demands that the material for the eucharistic celebration appear as actual food. (GIRM, no. 283)

This is a statement about texture, shape, taste, even smell. Because this statement is juxtaposed with the requirement that the bread be unleavened and with the instructions in other documents that it be made from wheat flour and water only, there is a great challenge. Some ignore the instruction that the bread "appear as actual food" and continue to use thin wafers. Others ignore the restrictions on ingredients. Still others insist that we can live with both instructions—though not without some effort. Some have devised recipes for such bread and have created a ministry of bread baking in the parish (see one such recipe on page 78). Some have sought out places that offer mass-produced (excuse the pun) breads, but with greater size, texture and taste to them (see the addresses on page 65).

2. *The bread, at least some of it, is to be in large pieces so that it can be broken publicly.* This is inconvenient in the way liturgy is often inconvenient. Note especially that the instruction (GIRM, no. 283) states that the pieces of the large bread are for distribution to the assembly. They are not all to be used for the presider's own communion nor are they ever to be

History of the Cup

For the first six centuries of Christian eucharistic life, communion in both kinds, the eucharistic bread and the cup, was considered both normal and desirable. Sharing in the cup in these earliest Christian generations was a simple, direct and natural response to the directive "take and drink." Typically, the deacon ministering the cup handed it to the standing communicant, who drank directly from it and returned it to the deacon. The deacon handed it to the next communicant, and so on.

During this early period there were some dissenters to the church's communion practice. But the dissenters were not objecting to communion from the cup. What they desired was to change the contents of the cup. Some made the case for water; others preferred milk. The official church insisted on wine.

Why? A too simple explanation is that the eucharist of the Lord's supper was celebrated with wine. That explanation begs the question. Wine—not water nor milk—was on the table when Jesus and his disciples gathered on the night before he died because of what wine signified humanly and religiously. In every century, in every culture, wine has signified solemnity, celebration, the marking of a special occasion even for those who are regularly at table together as family or friends. Wine is also a bond among pilgrims and strangers seeking to become community even for a short time.

In the ordinary celebrations of Jesus' day wine was also a religious symbol, an expression of faith and hope in God. A special ritual drinking from the cup at a gathering of believers was the focus of intense remembering. With the cup the people proclaimed their past and present and future in God, as this had been revealed to them by the great prophets and teachers of Israel. Jesus, too, gave his disciples the cup to drink as the way of remembering their past, present and future in him. Then he told them, "Do this for remembering until I come." Both the human and religious meanings of the cup known to Jesus and learned from him remain cogent.

In the circumstances of Catholic church life from the sixth to the 16th centuries, two major developments occurred which interfered with the power of the cup sign. The first broke the laity's relationship to the cup. The second made the desire for the cup a sign of disobedience to the Lord. Overcoming Catholic reluctance to give or to take the cup as an essential sacramental act will demand first a conscious advertence to the process which negated the sign of the cup. Only then can pastoral liturgists take on the task of reestablishing this aspect of eucharistic liturgy for the Catholic community.

The abandonment of the sign of the eucharistic cup did not occur in a single generation. James Megivern has recounted the gradual erosion of the sign over a span of many centuries in his scholarly work *Concomitance and Communion: A Study in Eucharistic Doctrine and Practice* (New York: Herder and Herder, 1963). One of the first deviations from the original and straightforward ritual action of taking and drinking was the practice of dipping the bread into the cup and doling out the moistened morsels to the laity. Like many other ritual corruptions of the early medieval period, this change was motivated by a growing obsession with human sinfulness and the emergence of a clerical class to

held (during the invitation to communion) in such a way that the presider seems to have pieced the broken bread together.

3. *The bread for communion is bread from this Mass.* This assembly has joined in the eucharistic prayer over this bread and this cup. These are then shared in holy communion. To do otherwise is to depart from the explicit instruction of the missal and from good liturgical sense (see the discussion of the rubrics on page 76). No one is to approach the tabernacle before communion. Only if the number has been miscalculated and there are not enough pieces of the bread—and this is seen too late for the pieces to be broken further—should anyone go to the tabernacle for eucharistic bread from another liturgy. This is not a difficult thing to do. Most parishes have a fairly consistent number of communicants at the same Mass each Sunday. Even seasonal variations can be taken into considera-

mediate between God and the merely baptized. At first, communion in two kinds was maintained through this altered form of communion by intinction. Ritual spoons and reeds also appeared. But the laity were not allowed to take and drink.

At the close of the 11th century local European synods had judged that communion in two kinds should remain the norm for the laity unless necessity or caution demanded the contrary. This was, in a very real sense, a quite traditional norm. (The earliest Christian generations had provided for the single species of wine only, for example, for the communion of the sick or infants.) But in the 11th century what necessity and caution seemed to demand in the matter of the laity's communion was filtered through the great medieval preoccupations with identifying and distinguishing things sacred and profane. The baptized laity who played secular to the clergy's sacred received communion only infrequently. When they did, conscious efforts were made to dissuade them of any need for directly

approaching the cup. By the end of the 13th century, the species of wine was formally prohibited by law for anyone but the priest celebrant.

Controversy over the issue whether the Lord intended the laity also to take and drink raged and smoldered from the 14th to the 16th centuries. The Council of Trent formally ruled in the mid-16th century that the chalice was properly to be reserved for the clergy. Some pastoral concessions were made for a time. But the great Jesuit apologist Peter Canisius expressed the prevailing sentiment with his declaration that the enemies of the church could be recognized by the usage of the chalice.

Vatican II in a single sentence restored the chalice to the laity in principle, leaving to the bishops the right to establish norms for actual reintroduction of the eucharistic cup to the laity.

Excerpts from "Historical Perspectives," by Mary Collins. Reprinted from *It Is Your Own Mystery*, pp. 11–13. Copyright © 1977, The Liturgical Conference, Washington, D.C. All rights reserved. Used with permission.

tion. The ministry of the sacristan is extremely helpful here in preparing the right measure of bread for each liturgy, labeling these measures or actually putting them in place before the Mass. Consistent problems with too little or too much bread should be remedied by increasing or decreasing the standard amount. This implies also that those pieces to be broken are premarked to be broken into a set number of pieces or that all who preside and all ministers of communion share an understanding of the number of small pieces to come from each large piece of bread.

These are not insignificant matters. We are easily inclined to spend time and money on the furnishings and decor of our churches or on the programs of education and charity. This is all to the good. It should strike us as very strange when a parish that has worked hard to have a fine physical facility and strong parish activities and outreach can gather on Sunday with no thought whatsoever to the quality and meaning of the bread (or the wine). Is it that we believe that nothing matters except that the bread be consecrated? But the truth is, for us, that this bread must bear the weight of our whole baptized selves, must somehow manifest the truth about this church in a way that can draw us endlessly to the Lord. The bread is not, has never been, the rich and magnificent breads humans have baked. It is always a poor bread, a bread of the poor. But it is bread!

Vessels

In a eucharistic celebration, the vessels for the bread and wine deserve attention and care. Just as in other types of celebration those objects which are central in the rite are a natural focus. When the eucharistic assembly is large, it is desirable not to have the additional plates and cups necessary for communion on the altar. A solution is to use one large breadplate and either one large chalice or a large flagon until the breaking of the bread. At the fraction, any other chalices or plates needed are brought to the altar. While the bread is broken on sufficient plates for sharing, the ministers of the cups pour from the flagon into the communion chalices. The number and design of such vessels will depend on the size of the community they serve. To eat and drink is the essence of the symbolic fullness of this sacrament. Communion under one kind is an example of the minimizing of primary symbols.

The pouring should be done with reverence and a fullness that is shown by lifting up the cup that is being filled.

Likewise, to rely on bread from the tabernacle is to tear apart the eucharistic action of this assembly, to deny the human difference it makes when a church has finally learned to join in a eucharistic prayer. The constant practice of the church has been that bread consecrated at this eucharist is to be consumed at this eucharist: A presider could never receive communion from the tabernacle while putting into the tabernacle all the bread of the Mass. That has been the church's teaching and practice—now we must see the grace and the logic of applying it to all the assembly.

Many of the supplementary materials on these pages are discussions of the reasons for and the practice of communion under both kinds. Many of the practical issues—from the storage of wine to the concern with AIDS—are treated in detail. It is a sign of how off-balance we have become that so much effort has to go into arguing for this fullness of communion.

The sacramentary puts the matter directly:

> The sign of communion is more complete when given under both kinds, since the sign of the eucharistic meal appears more clearly. The intention of Christ that the new and eternal covenant be ratified in his blood is better expressed, as is the relation of the eucharistic banquet to the heavenly banquet. (GIRM, no. 240)

Communion from the cup is, as so many parishes have discovered, a practice that is realistic for every Sunday liturgy. It can be introduced with good catechesis of the assembly and careful training of the ministers. Any initial discouragement is passing. Two things especially bring people eventually to the cup: first, simply the fact that the cup is always present; second, the gentleness and care with which it is

The Body *and* Blood of Christ

So that this "fuller light" may fall upon the import of Christ's words at the Last Supper and in the eucharistic prayer, and for the sake of the faithful's greater participation in the mystery, communion under both kinds is to be desired in all celebrations of the Mass, although this is not possible in all cases. For in this sacred rite "the sign of the eucharistic meal stands out more explicitly," and the act of drinking the consecrated wine, the Blood of Christ, strengthens the faith of the communicants in the sacrificial nature of the Mass. Communion under both kinds can therefore manifest more fully the nature of the Mass both as a sacrifice and as a sacred banquet, ritually expressing that "the sacrifice and the sacred Meal belong to the same mystery, to such an extent that they are linked to one another by a very close theological and sacramental bond."

offered by attentive ministers. If the whole of the rite is carefully planned (then evaluated and corrected) and if ministers are both reverent and confident, the numbers approaching the cup will increase. As this happens, the careful sacristan will be increasing the amount of wine normally provided for each Sunday liturgy.

The minister who pours from the larger container (a beautiful pitcher or flagon) into the cups should do so with both reverence and dignity. Haste is unnecessary. Awkwardness is a distraction. This is a gesture to be rehearsed in the course of becoming a minister of communion. Periodically, the ministers may need a bit of a refresher course. The tray

Preparation of the Vessels

From experience careful judgments should be made before the celebration of each Mass that enough bread and wine are made ready for the communication of the faithful in a particular eucharistic liturgy. Wine may not be consecrated at one Mass and reserved for use at another.

The wine should be placed in flagons or pitchers of careful design and quality as befits the celebration of the eucharistic mystery. The bread should be placed on one large paten or plate, or in a ciborium in the style of a bowl appropriate as a container of bread. The vessels should be sturdy, made of materials which are solid and nonabsorbent. Preference is always to be given to materials that do not break easily or become unusable. Before being used, vessels for the celebration must be blessed by the bishop or priest according to the Rite of Blessing of a Chalice and Paten.

Use is not to be made of simple baskets or other receptacles meant for ordinary use outside of the sacred celebrations, nor are the sacred vessels to be of poor quality or lacking any artistic merit.

When the altar is prepared after the general intercessions the wine may be brought forward in one chalice or, when the assembly is very large, one chalice and as many flagons as are necessary. Only one chalice (and the requisite number of flagons) and one large paten, ciborium or similar vessel should be on the altar during the rites of preparation up to and including the rite of the fraction when other empty chalices and ciboria may be brought to the altar. At that time the consecrated bread is placed in several ciboria or on plates and the consecrated wine is poured into enough chalices for use in the Rite of Communion. It should be remembered that enough eucharistic bread should be consecrated for each Mass.

Excerpts from *This Holy and Living Sacrifice: Directory for the Celebration and Reception of Communion under Both Kinds*, nos. 39–42. Copyright © 1985, United States Catholic Conference. All rights reserved. Used with permission.

with the cups should also contain a purificator for each cup. These can be placed where the individual ministers who come forward to take a cup can also take a purificator without awkwardly reaching in front of the one doing the pouring.

"Take this, all of you, and drink from it." These words were not taken seriously by Roman Catholics for many centuries. Yet the Roman Catholic church never put the cup entirely aside. It was always there for the presider, at least. That much was done as we somehow clung to the conviction that both eating and drinking are meant to take place at this paschal meal. The presence of the cup for the assembly at every liturgy allows us the fullness of the symbol. To drink from the cup is to find and to proclaim this covenant in the blood of Jesus, to find and to proclaim delight and suffering at the very same moment.

In 1985, the National Conference of Catholic Bishops published *This Holy and Living Sacrifice: Directory for the Celebration and Reception of Communion under Both Kinds.* This brief text should be consulted for both the theology and the pastoral practice of communion. Selections from this document appear on pages 46 and 47.

ORDERLY PROCEDURES

Every parish must find the best way for good order as bread is broken, wine poured and the ministers sent to their stations. How many ministers are necessary? The answer is in terms of the number of people present and the number of stations possible for an orderly procession. The ideal is not getting the communion over with as soon as possible, but rather having enough ministers that there can be a sense of unity in the communion. Space is the other control; when at all possible, all communion stations should be located to bring people forward and close to the table.

When most of those who take the eucharistic bread approach the cup also, then two ministers of the cup will be needed for each minister of bread.

The nature of the sign demands that the material for the eucharistic celebration appear as actual food.

GENERAL INSTRUCTION
OF THE ROMAN MISSAL

How do the ministers know where to take up their stations? Each parish must devise its own way of dealing with this. To leave it for the moment is to court confusion. There are several ways that have proven effective. Under the first, the ministers are asked to come about 15 minutes before the liturgy and to sign in. The sign-in board or paper will assign them a place and will indicate which minister is to do the pouring, which to assist the presider in breaking the bread and filling the plates. Each team of ministers has a leader who watches this process of signing in. Just before the liturgy begins, this person tries to fill any slots left empty by the failure of some assigned ministers to appear. Communion ministers who are not assigned on a given Sunday can be asked to stop by the sign-in place before going to their places in the assembly.

Some parishes have used another method of assigning ministers to particular stations. Each vessel (cup or plate) is designated for a specific station. The problem here is doing this without unsightly tags taped to the vessels. Vessels made especially for the parish by a potter or metalsmith could include small letters or Roman numerals to designate the various stations. Yet another method involves the assignment of each individual to a fixed station for the duration of a given schedule. This works well when the ministers function in teams and when there are few substitutions and few absentees.

A very simple way of avoiding confusion is establishing a set practice: The first person to take a cup from the altar goes to the south station, the next person goes to the middle station, the one who has been filling the cups takes the last cup and goes to the north station. This is the way it is done, every time. (This becomes somewhat more difficult to apply when the ministers stay as a body at the altar until after the invitation: "This is the Lamb of God . . ." In that case they are all taking their vessels at the same time and confusion follows.)

MINISTERS OF COMMUNION

What qualities ought a minister of communion to possess? The one at the source of any others, the one supporting the whole ministry, would be this: A minister of communion should be one who knows what it means to say, "The body of Christ," "The blood of Christ."

After that, they should be persons who can handle the practical things of the rite well: coming forward to the table, standing around the altar, pouring and breaking, carrying cup or plate, attending individually to each communicant.

As a group, the ministers of communion should manifest all the diversity of the larger parish.

Ministers of communion wear no distinctive vesture or symbol. They are expected to dress in an appropriate manner. They do not walk in the procession at the beginning of Mass nor in the recessional. They sit with the assembly and have no area designated for them. In some cases the adult acolytes at Sunday Mass will fittingly serve as ministers of the eucharist. (In fact, the ministry of communion is acolyte work.) In this case, the acolyte–minister of communion will wear whatever is customary for adult acolytes.

AT THE INVITATION of the presider, the assembly has recited or sung the Lord's Prayer. At the invitation of the deacon or presider, the assembly has exchanged the sign of peace. All have been singing the Lamb of God from the time the presider lifted up the whole bread to be broken until the breaking and pouring have been completed and the communion ministers stand at their stations. The sacramentary suggests that there may be a few moments of silence before the invitation to communion: "The priest prepares to receive the body and blood of Christ by praying quietly. The faithful also do this by praying in silence." (GIRM, no. 56) This would not be a lengthy silence but a matter of a pause, almost like taking a deep breath between the preparation and the deed.

Now there is another invitation. The presider lifts up the bread. Note that it is the bread the presider is showing to the assembly, not the plate. Note also that this is not the same gesture as that which accompanied the end of the eucharistic prayer ("Through him, with him, in him . . ."), but rather it is a gesture of invitation. The rubrics do not direct the presider to lift up the cup also, but this would seem entirely appropriate.

Looking directly at the assembly, the presider speaks this final invitation of the communion rite. Concerning the words of the invitation, Robert Hovda writes:

Even the most conservative interpreters of liturgical law have suggested areas of "explicit" and of "implicit" personal creativity with regard to the texts of the *Ordo Missae*. The introduction to communion is one of the areas of implicitly encouraged creativity, according to an article by G. Fontaine in *Notitiae*, May 1972 (Roman Congregation for the Sacraments and Divine Worship) and in *Newsletter of the U.S. Bishops' Committee on the Liturgy*, July/August 1972: "I believe that it must be clearly established that the introductory texts in the *Ordo Missae* are not *'ne varietur'* texts . . . but they are models or examples for inspiration to be adapted to the genius of the vernacular and the needs of diverse assemblies." *It Is Your Own Mystery* (Washington: The Liturgical Conference, 1977), page 27.

The length, the tone and the quality of the text offered in the sacramentary must be taken as a model for any variation. A text for Advent might be:

This is the Lamb of God
who takes away the sins of the world,
the Ruler who now draws near.
Happy are those who are called to the Lord's supper.

The Common Cup: Putting Aside the Fears

Such is the progress of our conciliar reform and renewal that many Catholic parishes have not yet got around to offering the common cup regularly in eucharistic celebrations. Even sadder is the fact that, pleading the AIDS epidemic, some of those who had made progress in this important matter are now turning back. At least, that is what I hear. I am sure it is a small number, but we cannot afford even that much recidivism. The reactionary cultural temper of the present moment, the evident nostalgia of much current church leadership for a less troublesome ear, the repugnance of many clergy with regard to the time and effort ("bother") good liturgical celebration requires—all these unlovely traits of the time have made it much too easy for a thoughtless reaction under the guise of a health concern.

Ever since the timid and hesitant conciliar restoration of "bready" bread and the common chalice for the entire eucharistic assembly, Catholics have experienced a remarkable reawakening to the primary character of the eucharist, which is, of course, its meal character, its character as a glimpse of the heavenly banquet, the reign of God, the meaning and purpose and goal of all creation. After our long detour and focus on secondary aspects of the eucharist, this attention to its primary meaning and to the consequent diminishment of the ritual symbol when part of the assembly neglects to eat and drink

in common at Christ's table has begun to rescue us from a serious distortion and twisting of Jesus Christ's last will and testament: The Lord's Supper.

Ritual in general thrives as common gesture, movement, action. It languishes to the extent these things are not common in the celebrating assembly. When the particular ritual action in question is central and climactic, like holy communion, these principles become crucial. While it seems to me a masterpiece of understatement, the *General Instruction of the Roman Missal* is unambiguous:

The sign of communion is more complete when given under both kinds, since in that form the sign of the eucharistic meal appears more clearly. The intention of Christ that the new and eternal cove-nant be ratified in his blood is better expressed, as is the relation of the eucharistic banquet to the heavenly banquet. . . . The faithful should be urged to take part in the rite which brings out the sign of the eucharistic meal more fully. (240–41)

That is a clear statement of repentance by the church for that period of liturgical decadence during which the common chalice ceased to be a normal part of the communion experience of believers in the Sunday assembly. It was during this time also that the eucharist came to be regarded chiefly as an object rather than as an action. James Megivern says of this eucharistic tangent:

As an object to be looked at and adored, the species of bread had a distinct advantage. It could be made into attractive form, stamped with an image of Christ or the Cross, and encased in precious holders for display, all of which helped the pious imagination to see Christ present much as he had been in Bethlehem, merely reduced to somewhat smaller dimensions. The species of wine did not lend itself to similar treatment very readily, since it was much harder or at least less satisfying to try to imagine a cup of liquid in personal terms. The miracle-hosts (stories of "bleeding" breads from the eleventh to the sixteenth century) could only increase this approach. As long as such an unsacramental outlook prevailed among parts of the Christian populace, communion under both species could hardly be expected to be much insisted upon even when it was maintained. *Concomitance and Communion: A Study in Eucharistic Doctrine and Practice* (New York: Herder and Herder, 1963), p. 45.

"Take, all of you, and eat it. . . . Take, all of you, and drink from it. . . ." It is as simple as that. The eucharistic sacrament is one of eating and drinking commonly (all of us, each unique and different, sexes, colors, ages, conditions, classes, types) the same holy bread, the same holy wine, one plate, one cup of Christ. One could truncate the sacrament for the benefit of an infant after baptism, or for the benefit of an adult hospitalized, shut-in or imprisoned. But to truncate the sacrament in the midst of the Sunday assembly and in the course of its celebration was inconceivable until both rite and faith were in sharp decline.

Megivern's study shows that Christians accustomed to the full symbolic action resisted all attempts to reduce this fullness, whether the plea was efficiency or any other reason. The Roman Church, particularly, held out for the full symbolic value—the entire assembly's eating from the common plate and drinking from the common cup in two distinct actions. "For nearly 12 centuries it was the vigilance of Rome that rejected every move that tried to 'institutionalize' any other form of communion except under the two separate species as done by Christ." (p. 242) "In the eyes of Rome, to concede to the difficulties of the chalice by resorting to intinction was little different from dropping the chalice altogether." (pp. 35–36)

When one drinks from the common chalice properly administered, the safeguards are many: (1) the agency of the wine's alcoholic content, (2) cups with a polished metal surface, (3) the minister's careful wiping of the rim, inside and out, and the turning of the cup slightly after each communicant.

Another occasional objection has to do with the "danger" that drinking from the chalice presents to alcoholics. Again, one sympathizes with the motive for the objection, but an imagined danger is a poor challenge to the full sign value of the eucharist. I am an alcoholic, and with the help of many others like myself I have refrained from alcoholic beverages for more than ten years, to my great benefit. But I have participated fully in holy communion all this while, taking the slightest sip from the communion chalice. Touching one's lips to the wine, sufficiently to taste it and absorb a few drops, is certainly a real participation in the cup. One need not take a draught and an alcoholic should not. In all this time, I have experienced no ill effect, no trace of an aroused craving or compulsion. This kind of careful participation in no way contradicts the sound principle that alcoholics must never take that first drink.

Excerpts from "The Amen Corner," by Robert Hovda. Reprinted from *Worship*, vol. 60, no. 1, pp. 67–71. Copyright © 1986, Robert W. Hovda. Used with permission.

For Christmastime:

> *This is the Lamb of God*
> *who takes away the sins of the world,*
> *Emmanuel, God-with-us.*
> *Happy are those who are called to the Lord's supper.*

For Lent and Eastertime:

> *This is the Lamb of God*
> *by whose blood we are cleansed,*
> *by whose wounds we are healed.*
> *Happy are those who are called to the Lord's supper.*

These texts are only a phrase longer than the standard text. The added words are taken from other parts of the seasonal liturgies (the liturgy of the hours is an excellent source). Thus, in adapting the words of invitation:

- Maintain the approximate length.
- Use words that are well-crafted and echo the scriptures.
- Memorize the words so they can be spoken directly to the assembly.
- Use the same text at all parish Masses throughout a season or a period of Ordinary Time.
- Always end with the same line so that the assembly can respond.

Often a presider will change the final line to "Happy are we . . ." One can understand the reasons, but there are strong arguments to be made for maintaining the use of "those." "Those" is inclusive of "we," but unlike "we" it is not so limited.

The sacramentary says explicitly that the presider is to speak the response with the assembly.

COMMUNION

The presider then takes communion. The words "May the body of Christ . . ." and "May the blood of Christ . . ." are to be inaudible. Like the prayer before communion ("Lord Jesus Christ"), these are prayers of the individual. In catechesis, they can be offered to children, catechumens and other adults as part of the tradition's vocabulary of prayer.

The communion song "begins when the priest receives communion" (GIRM, no. 56). Thus it begins immediately after the invitation and response. But if the song begins, so should the procession. That is possible if the ministers are in place, as described previously, and if the procession has already taken shape. The presider then joins the ministers immediately after receiving communion. It is important that the presider sometimes bring the plate and bread and sometimes the cup.

All *Receive* Communion

In the eighth-century *Ordines romani*, a deacon brings communion to the pope at his throne, the archdeacon or a subdeacon gives him the chalice, then the bishops and presbyters come up to receive the consecrated bread from the pope's hand. One of the bishops or presbyters gives the chalice to the other bishops, presbyters, and deacons, and a deacon in turn gives the chalice to the lesser orders. Then the people receive the bread from the pope or from the bishops and presbyters, and the deacons administer the chalice. In a word, everyone *receives* communion from someone else. No one just *takes* it. . . .

But as is often the case in matters liturgical, it is the East-Syrian or Nestorian Church of Persia that reflects the earliest usage and best understanding of what it is all about. Canon 2 of Catholicos Mar Iso'yahb I (518–596) prescribes the rite of communion of the ministers. The presbyter who has been chosen to consecrate the sacrament receives first, even before the bishop:

. . . The bishop, if he is present, gives it [the consecrated bread] to him; if he is not present, the senior priest in order of precedence gives it to him. And in turn, he who consecrates gives it to the one who gave it to him. And it should be done likewise for the chalice of the Lord. He who has consecrated gives communion to the priests and deacons who are in the sanctuary . . . Then the priests distribute communion . . .

The anonymous ninth-century *Commentary on the Ecclesiastical Offices* attributed to George of Arbela has the same usage, and tells us why: salvation is something mediated to us by Our Lord. So even the priest, who as the Lord's image is himself a mediator of salvation to others, must receive it from another.

Excerpts from *Beyond East & West: Problems in Liturgical Understanding*, by Robert Taft, SJ, pp. 102–103, 105. Copyright © 1984, The Pastoral Press, Washington, D.C. All rights reserved. Used with permission.

Normally, the minister with the cup should be some distance from the minister of the bread and should be turned to face the latter. This allows for those who do not choose to receive from the cup to pass by others who are waiting their turn. Reception from the cup normally follows the reception of the bread, simply maintaining the order of the presider's communion.

Every person, except the presider, is to receive the bread and cup from another person. This includes the communion ministers themselves. The cup is never left to be taken up from the altar or another place by the communicant.

Robert Hovda writes thus of the distribution of communion:

> The moment of communion is one that should be seized by both the minister and the communicant. There are plenty of moments in the liturgy when ministers are attentive to the congregation as a corporate entity. This is one moment when attention should be individual and total. The eyes of the minister should meet the eyes of the communicant. The minister says the words of the formula *to* each person (not to the air). . . . In placing the holy bread on the palm of the communicant's hand, the minister will touch that hand. The same will be true of the minister of the cup. *Eye contact, direct address, touching!* All are part of the experience of sharing. . . . This means that there can be no rush. One can minister communion with reverence and dignity and personal attention and still keep the procession moving steadily. But it cannot be done in haste, or with absentmindedness, or with frantic searchings of the approaching processional lines. *It Is Your Own Mystery,* page 32.

To speak of the skills to be developed in the minister of communion, presiders included, is to speak of developing this manner for every person in the procession.

We search for, we need, the fullness of this communion. That need is why communion from the cup is becoming the normal manner of celebrating the communion rite. That need for full expression of the symbol is also the reason why that manner of communion called intinction is to be avoided. As done by the minister (dipping the bread into the cup and then giving it to the communicant), this practice has almost

Our Thirst for Communion

A May 6, 1988, story in the *New York Times* reported:

Human saliva contains substances that prevent the AIDS virus from infecting white blood cells, a new study has found. The researchers said the finding might help explain why no cases have been documented in which the AIDS virus was transmitted from person to person through saliva . . . Dr. Philip Fox of the National Institute of Dental Research in Bethesda, Maryland, who led the research group, said the results were "in keeping with the epidemiological evidence." While some studies have found minute levels of AIDS virus in saliva of virus carriers, studies of the spread of AIDS have failed to find that it is transmitted by kissing or other saliva contact.

For example, family members who shared toothbrushes and kissed AIDS patients did not become infected. The protective substances in saliva may be "one of the mechanisms by which the body protects itself," Dr. Fox said. He added that saliva is well known to contain substances that kill bacteria and funguses and so he is not surprised that saliva also blocks the AIDS virus.

When it comes to sharing the cup, we are all entitled to concern for our health and the health of others. What seems so strange is the selectivity of the concern. We worry about sharing a common cup but not about sharing a common world. We wonder what diseases our ("Peace be with you") neighbor in the pew might have left for us on the cup's rim, but we have an awful record of ignoring what is far more real, the ecological havoc we continue to inflict on the earth and its present poorer inhabitants and future inhabitants (our kids). Toxic wastes only excite us when the cancer rate on our block shoots up. Concern about little things like the throw-away containers the hamburgers come in (those squeaky plastic boxes that will still be around—no decay, no burning—at the second coming) may occasionally rise to the surface, but on the whole we are a people terribly slow to take real healthiness seriously. Why then do so many pass by the cup? Steeled as we all are to the unhealthy deeds of waste disposal, pesticide spraying, acid rain and even chemical warfare, what is so scary about that cup?

Is it perhaps that here—far more than in the very separate pieces of bread—we confront a very specific kind of intimacy? Fear of contagion is certainly part of resisting the cup, but is not fear of such intimacy the larger context? (On this subject, see "AIDS and the Cup" by Gordon Lathrop, *Worship,* March 1988.) A people's rituals do not have to go after expressions of intimacy in any artificial or planned manner. Such expressions will be there by their nature. Our rituals are the ways we learn to be ourselves. If solidarity is vital to our communal identity, then the ritual rehearses us in solidarity. So smoking a common pipe or drinking from a common cup are deep and widespread ritual expressions. And they don't need intricate theologies to convey their profound task. Just being there and taking part will do quite well, thank you.

This sharing of a cup, for Christians at eucharist, does have to do with solidarity and thus intimacy. The latter should not be confused with coziness, comfort, the tight little group. Our intimacy is not

disappeared. However, it remains common for a person to receive the bread, then to approach the minister of the cup and to dip the bread into the wine. Often this has to do with a fear of drinking from the common cup. Careful teaching and example should be employed to discourage such a distortion of the sign of the meal. The minister with the cup, of course, must show the same manner to all, including those who choose not to drink but to dip the eucharistic bread into the cup.

When the number of communicants is large, the best practice is to have an additional minister of communion assigned, one who has no

that of the family or the club. Strangely, it means strangers. Even in the tiny rural or inner-city parish, where everyone *does* know everyone, it still means an intimacy with strangers—in the sense that this sharing in the blood of Christ is bond to all who ever drank this cup, but also in the sense that this starkly physical thing *is* intimate.

Even if I know all these other people, here is something we just don't do elsewhere. However well we know each other, in this culture we don't let it lead to common drinking vessels. Except here. At the level of vessels, we are strangers. Except here. The deed of drinking does not somehow replace strangers with intimates, but it shows how things are meant in this assembly: Somehow our bonds with one another, friends and strangers, make us neither friends nor strangers. That particular intimacy, that solidarity, is very hard for us. We are comfortable with real intimates, comfortable with strangers, but we are distinctly *un*comfortable with the relationship suggested by the communal cup. We walk by, not inflicting our mouths and tongues on others.

And what we miss! The starting point for any catechesis is invitation *to* something, is somebody's excitement: "Take this, all of you, and drink . . ." We need to reflect, individually and perhaps sometimes as a parish staff or as a liturgy committee or in any small group, on the thoughts and the images and the emotions and the prayers and the convictions each of us has on moving toward the cup, taking and drinking. I don't mean only the momentary feelings, but how the deed itself, done consciously, has done something of ritual's work: given us a glimpse of the reign of God, showed us how to walk there, how to be among others, how to sip what is at once festive and bitter.

Little practical things also help in quietly inviting greater participation in the cup. Is the central cup reserved for the presider or is it too shared by the assembly? It should be shared. Does the presider always take a plate with the consecrated bread to the distribution of holy communion, or does the presider just as often take a cup (thus giving a very strong message)? How have the ministers of the cup come to understand their service to the assembly and what example do they themselves give of partaking from the cup reverently? Do other ministers, especially the ushers, partake of the cup? Have they been encouraged to do so? All in all, we need to know why this is so important.

Excerpts from "Many Other Things," by Gabe Huck. Reprinted from *Liturgy 80*, July 1988, p. 15.

station. When this is done, some of the consecrated wine is left in the large vessel on the altar and some of the holy bread is left on a plate on the altar. It is the task of the extra minister to attend to the needs of those distributing communion. In the case of the bread, this minister can notice that the lines are particularly long at one station or the other and can bring additional bread to the minister long before that minister has to worry about breaking pieces in two or returning to the table for more. In the case of the cup, the extra minister can take the pitcher from station to station about halfway through the communion. With the cup, it is important not to wait until the last minute because communicants take tinier and tinier sips as the amount decreases. It is far better to have a good amount so that people will not feel that they need to ration it for the sake of those who follow them. A deacon assisting with the liturgy may well be the best one to take on this role of servant to the communion ministers.

A TRUE PROCESSION

This is the most difficult and yet crucial part of preparing the rite of communion for a parish. It is difficult because of architecture and furniture, old habits and low expectations. It is crucial because

---

The Goodness of Bread

Have you ever tasted any of the breads of India? They're flat as paper or puffed as balloons. They're made from chickpea, millet, barley, lentil, wheat, rice or any combination of flours. They're fried, spit roasted, baked on hot rocks or even slapped to the sides of ovens. During most of the history of Europe the word "bread" meant just about the same thing that bread means in India today. There was infinite variety. Grains and legumes, any seed capable of being ground into a flour, made up the bulk of human diet. It was a diet nutritionists urge us to embrace again.

WHEAT FLOUR BREADS

Gluten is an organic compound most heavily concentrated in what we usually call "white flour" (wheat flour with the bran removed). Gluten enables

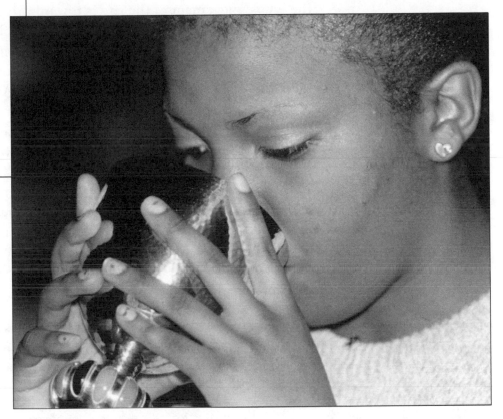

This sharing of a cup has to do with solidarity and intimacy. The deed itself gives us a glimpse of the reign of God, shows us how to be among others.

dough to form the structure unique to wheat breads and pasta. If you want the flour of any other grain or legume to form the structure we Westerners associate with bread, you have to add this gluten-rich white flour. Even rye or whole wheat breads often turn out like rocks without the addition of white flour.

The customary wedding "cake" in Sweden is simply a flat wafer, a token of an era when white flour was so rare it was only eaten in its most frugal form. A hundred years ago baked goods made solely with white flour were served only on holidays, weddings and funerals. Such breads or cakes were usually named a variant of the root word *kala*. Through linguistic shifts from "k" to "h" to "w," *kala* is the root of the words "whole," "health," "well," "wheel," "yule," "coil" and "calendar." It's a root which has been used in other languages for circle dances, kings, crowns and even Christmas. It's a royal word which evokes images of beauty, completeness, fulfillment and the kingdom of God, especially among breadbakers: festive Czech *kolacky*, Russian Easter *kulich*, Yiddish sabbath *challah*, and Greek funeral *kolliva*.

the whole movement of the rite is toward this moment. If we come this far and then can manage only a lot of individuals lining up, then—to put it in the terms of the *Constitution on the Sacred Liturgy*—we have fallen far short of the full, conscious and active participation that is to be the indispensable source of the Christian spirit. At this moment, above all others, the personal and the communal are one. The sign is that of the paschal banquet, of the church, of the communion of saints. But it has no existence apart from this assembly: how it sounds, moves, speaks and attends to the business at hand.

A procession is the movement of a group, the assembly in this case. We have all experienced processions. And we have all experienced lining up. They are quite different. It isn't the numbers. There can be 30 persons in a true procession and 100 in a mere line. What makes the difference? One thing is a sense that we are acting together. At the bank you may stand behind someone for some time, then have your turn, then

Wheat was once the grain of banquets, the flour of royalty, the bread of the kingdom. It is no wonder that it came to be the only grain used for the eucharistic meal, for the Jewish sabbath meal and for the Passover seder. Barley and rye might suffice for ordinary days, but on the Sabbath and the Lord's Day everyone was to eat white wheat flour bread like royalty, like wedding guests, like a people restored to health, to wellness, to wholeness.

In the churches of Western Europe, where wheat was rare, communion breads have generally been unleavened wafers. But the Eastern churches, living in the breadbasket of Eurasia, baked their communion breads with great lavishness using leavened bread, which is more spendthrift of flour than unleavened bread.

All this about wheat breads being said, we must quickly add that the mighty significance of wheat is only within a European and West Asian context. Even there, for all their high regard for the symbolism of wheat, this wheat bread was all too often absent from the tables of the very peasants who grew it for the wealthy. In the first centuries of the Common Era unleavened barley bread was eaten by poorer Jews at Passover. (Passover, after all, is celebrated during the season of the barley harvest.) Early Christian writers tell us that people brought their everyday breads for eucharist—certainly both barley and wheat breads, leavened and unleavened.

UNLEAVENED AND LEAVENED BREADS

The unleavened bread of Passover is called a bread of haste, a reminder that there was no time to wait for leavening to occur during the Exodus. People need an important reason *not* to leaven expensive wheat flour.

During the seder, unleavened bread is also called the bread of affliction, the bread of slaves. Herein

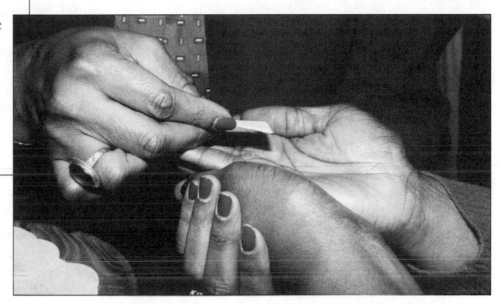

lies its most powerful meaning. Jewish law insists the bread of the seder be simple flour and water, without salt, eggs, oils or other enriching ingredients. Since the Middle Ages the church of the Roman rite has used only unleavened bread at eucharist. In one sense, this bread of affliction identifies our Mass as a paschal meal.

But what is leavening? Strictly speaking, leavening is anything—from carbonated water to yeast— which incorporates gas into dough to make it rise. Before packaged yeast, people kept their bread rising with sourdough. Lumps of sourdough, kept from one batch for the next, preserved the "living" part of bread. But sourdough has its drawbacks. After a while on the shelf, all sorts of other microbes begin to join the yeast in sourdough, so that it becomes a vile smelling stew. Throwing out this old leaven is a powerful symbol of getting rid of corruption. Note that the symbol of corruption isn't leaven, it's *old*

leaven (sourdough mixed with all sorts of corrupting organisms). Eating unleavened bread at Passover is the consequence of purging all the old leaven and starting anew. Read 1 Corinthians 5:6–8. Paul is not concerned with leaven but with *old* leaven, the stuff that stinks like death.

Fresh leaven is a symbol of the Spirit. In the Middle Ages leaven was called "goddisgoode," God's goodness, because of its miraculous ability to create raised loaves of bread. In Eastern Europe, under the influence of the Orthodox churches, Easter breads were baked as high as possible, as if God's Spirit had filled the unleavened bread of Passover with the very spirit of resurrection. In contrast, unleavened bread became lenten fare (like pretzels).

ALTAR BREADS

We wanted to share the recommendations of liturgy personnel around the country, so we conducted an

go your way. Each one did the same thing, and in turn, but each did it alone. At the liturgy you may stand behind someone for some time, then have your turn, then go your way. Each does the same thing, and in turn, but what we do is done as one. This is that banquet to which we have been called not as individuals but as the church. If it is the church approaching the table, then it ought to look like and sound like and act like the church. More will be said about the "sound like" later, for song is essential to the procession, but first the matter of the route.

How can that most intimate moment of the liturgy, the eating and drinking of each member, be given its true home within this manifestation of the church, its communion procession?

Most parishes made a transition some years ago from a communion practice that was simply for individuals to get up and crowd into the aisles and move forward. They asked the ushers to maintain an order, usually moving from the front pews to the back. This allowed an ordered

informal survey. We asked several people in various parts of the country what they use for altar breads in their own parishes, whether they were satisfied with it, and what they would recommend. The results were not surprising.

Most people unhesitatingly recommended home-baked loaves as their first choice. This ministry was worth the work, a true "liturgical act," a "labor of the people." One person said that the bread of eucharist should require a measure of inconvenience, a certain inexpediency, so the bread itself becomes a sign of the careful labor necessary for its production. Also, home-baked bread is more likely to appear as real food (as required by paragraph 283 of the *General Instruction of the Roman Missal*) and more likely to be in the form of one loaf, or at least large loaves which can be broken and shared (again, see paragraph 283). Larger loaves enable a worthy breaking of the bread, feasible in any parish. All our respondents regarded this breaking of large loaves as

an essential (yet often poorly handled) part of the communion rite. Breads, they felt, ought to be prepared to satisfy our rite rather than to keep for months in little plastic bags in the sacristy. Then liturgical norms would be better upheld and the communion rite could function as intended.

Storing home-baked altar breads is simple: Wrap them in air-proof material and store them in the freezer; even the refrigerator will keep breads for a month or more. Some breads are improved or deteriorate with freezing. Experiment with the bread you use. Bread should be served at room temperature, not right out of the refrigerator. Cold causes the natural oils to congeal, making the bread taste dry. Whole wheat flour itself has a high natural oil content, which means the flour is prone to rancidity. Store it dry and cold.

A few of our respondents mentioned using Arabic pita bread for eucharist. Pita gets its characteristic pocket from yeast; it is not an unleavened bread.

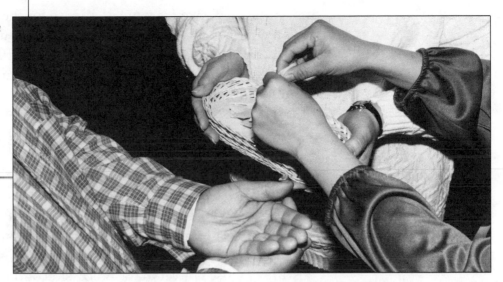

Neither is Armenian *lavash*. Just because a bread is dry or flat does not mean it's unleavened.

One person mentioned that flour manufacturers are required by the government to blend in several additives, are permitted to add certain ingredients to their flours and are further allowed a certain percentage of things which find their way into flour (things like insect parts, a reminder of our earthy existence). These "ingredients" of flours seem to confuse the liturgical proscription against additives. Of course, the same flour constituents are found in commercially baked breads as in home-baked breads.

A few altar bread recipes, along with most commercial altar bread bakers, achieve their wafer or soft textured breads through nonbiological leavening. No solid leavening agent is added, but air is kneaded into the dough or naturally carbonated water is used. A wafer gets its light texture by being made from a slurry of flour and water which is supercharged with air before baking. Jewish matzah is baked according to the strictest possible sense of "unleavened." During baking it is perforated with holes to release trapped gases, and it is baked until dry because any moisture will cause the growth of airborne yeast.

COMMERCIAL ALTAR BREADS

All in all, our respondents did not recommend commercially available altar breads, although most of them used commercial breads. However, the Santa Rita Abbey breads (HCR Box 929, Sonoita, Arizona 85637; 602/455-5595) received many compliments. They actually taste like bread! Another recommended supplier of breads and communion vessels is Meyer-Vogelpohl (717 Race Street, Cincinnati, Ohio 45202; 513/241-1535).

The purchaser of commercially available breads can go one of three routes: buying directly from a

movement and gave far more of a sense for the church approaching the table than when it was up to each individual to decide when to get up and crowd into the aisle. But usually we went no further. We were probably satisfying our drive for efficiency more than our desire to manifest our community.

The challenge is to look at the floor plan of the particular space where an assembly celebrates the liturgy and to think: How could we have a communion procession here? A procession is *not* the shortest distance between two points. It is about more than efficiency. It is not only about getting from the pew or chair to the communion minister. It is also about getting back. The whole is within the procession. What we are after here is a certain sense for what is happening: a paschal meal, our church at the Lord's table, all of us together. This has implications for the posture of those not yet in the procession or those who have finished the procession. Should people be kneeling or sitting or standing? Is it better practice for the procession and the posture of those in the pews to be linked, even as their voices are in the song? Then, when all have taken communion, comes the time of sitting or kneeling and quiet reflection.

commercial firm, buying through a religious goods store which deals wholesale with several companies, or buying from a religious community which either bakes its own breads or distributes breads baked elsewhere. The differences between the various commercial breads are subtle; thicknesses vary only a few millimeters. All appear more like wafers than breads. Just about every altar bread baker offers a choice between white or whole wheat. In addition, many commercial suppliers have specialty breads, perhaps a bit larger or thicker or chewier, which are not always listed in their brochures. A purchaser needs to ask specifically for samples of all their products.

Buying from a religious community is an important means of parish support for that community.

That alone may be reason enough to buy from them. Unfortunately, even religious communities cater to popular demand; this demand often does not include the larger, more substantial altar breads. Speak up.

For a fine discussion of the pertinent liturgical directives, as well as the history of liturgical breads, see "Eucharistic Bread: Actual Food," by J. Frank Henderson (*National Bulletin on Liturgy* [Canada], no. 69, May–June 1979, pp. 129–43) and "Bread and Wine," by John Huels (*Emmanuel*, November 1984, pp. 520–24).

Excerpts from "Bread," by Peter Mazar. Reprinted from *Liturgy 80*, July 1987, pp. 4–6.

But for any of this to be, there has to be some thinking about choreography within the floor plan.

We will look at five typical floor plans and see how a procession might happen in each.

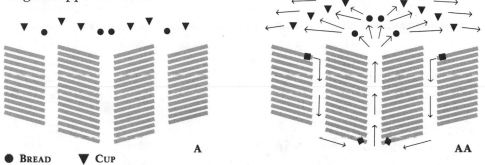

● Bread   ▼ Cup   A   AA

Plan A has a center aisle, side aisles and aisles along the walls (here the pews or benches have been angled to provide a greater sense of community within the assembly). The expectation would be for four communion stations (two of the ministers of bread together in the center). Those in the center sections would come to the ministers of bread at the center then turn to the ministers of the cup on either side, go on to the side aisles and back into the pews. Those in the front pews make just a little circle, those in the rear pews a large circle. Meanwhile, in each of the side sections, the procession begins with the front row, moving to the inside aisle, forward to the communion station, and back by way of the aisle against the far wall. All of this would be guided by four ushers: moving back from the front, keeping a good order, helping to raise kneelers, coming to communion themselves after everyone else.

How could the same space give us a true procession? Look at Plan AA, same design but different communion stations. Suppose the ushers were to go first up the side aisles and ask the persons sitting at the point designated ■ to follow them. Two ushers on each side would go together to this point. One would stay there, the other would lead the people of the front side pew back down the aisle (thus immediately persons from several of these side pews would have to get in the procession—that is the task of the usher who stayed behind), across behind the back pew of the center section, and up the center aisle to a communion

Altar Wine

The high sugar content of wine grapes makes possible the growth of natural yeasts, but retards the growth of many other organisms which would otherwise ruin the fruit. Once the grapes are crushed, the process of fermentation begins whereby these yeasts convert the sugars into alcohol. Eventually the alcohol kills the very yeast that generated it, stopping fermentation.

One remarkable quality about wine is that it is "living," improving or deteriorating as long as there is some exchange with the atmosphere. That's what the invention of the cork accomplished: Air slowly passes through it. Of course, screwtop caps undo all that.

"Living," however, does not always mean improving. Unlike distilled liquors with their higher alcohol content, and despite the exaggerated press given to the qualities of very old wines, most wines deteriorate markedly after a year or two. Keep that in mind when ordering in quantity. Unless you have the facilities to store wine optimally (cool, even temperatures and darkness), don't plan on storing wine over six months. Deterioration isn't always a subtle matter detectable only by sophisticated tongues; a long-forgotten bottle may have turned into costly vinegar.

THE LITURGICAL SYMBOLISM OF WINE

In the mind's eye the spirit of life has often been imagined as red and flowing, like blood and wine. Red is the color of May Day parades, lunar New Year greetings, Orthodox Easter eggs, Oriental birth announcements, and it is the most popular color of national flags worldwide. But doesn't wine come in other colors besides red? If you remove the skins immediately after crushing, regardless of the color of the grape, the juice will be white. But that's a relatively newfangled discovery. White or rosé wines were unknown to most people throughout history.

The color red is important if we are to appreciate the significance of wine in our tradition. The color associates wine with blood. In the covenant with Noah (Genesis 9:1–7), God forbids the consuming of blood. Since this prohibition against consuming blood was enjoined on all humanity, the council of Jerusalem saw fit to remind gentile Christians of their obligation to observe this commandment (Acts 15). Blood was called the seat of life (Leviticus 17). The drinking of blood supposedly filled a person with the living spirit of whatever animal (or human!) was slaughtered. This was regarded by Jews and early Christians as a particularly vile aspect of idol worship. In Judaism, even the killing of a chicken must be accomplished with utmost reverence, since blood contains the breath of God. Because of the sanctity of blood, its sprinkling was holy and central to worship in the Jerusalem temple.

Besides symbolizing life, wine is a symbol of joy and conviviality. Folks who enjoy wine around a common table, perhaps a bit tipsy, have all their defenses down. It's no surprise that wine therefore represents love, trust and fealty, and the corresponding notions of covenant and reconciliation. To drink a libation was synonymous with forming a treaty (Genesis 35:14). Again, in this sense, there is a link with the symbolism of blood as a sign of fidelity and

station. After receiving communion, each person would move to the aisle against the wall and back into the pew.

In the front area there are still four communion stations, but they are placed further back so that, as people come to the front of the center aisle, they can move toward either of two ministers of bread, then to any of three or four ministers of the cup.

When the last persons from the side sections have entered the procession (still moving back, behind the center section, up the center aisle), the usher follows the line until its last person has passed the back pew of the center section. The usher then brings the people of that pew into the procession (beginning at ♦), entering the center aisle and going forward to communion. Then the second aisle from the back of the center section, and so on.

---

salvation (Genesis, chapters 4, 8, 15 and 22; Exodus 12; 1 Peter 1; Revelation 7) and as a sign of forgiveness and atonement (Exodus 30:10, Numbers 19, Romans 3, Colossians 1, among many others).

Blood and, by association, wine signify bonds of kinship. To intermingle blood or to share a cup of wine creates "blood brothers and sisters" who become as interrelated as a grapevine and its branches. By equating a cup of wine with the blood of the new covenant, Jesus identifies this imagery of "blood relations" with the sharing of the cup.

One of the most profound meanings of wine is as a symbol of the Holy Spirit. It is no coincidence that alcoholic drinks are called "spirits." This symbolism is made delightfully clear in Acts 2. The disciples are accused of being filled with the new wine. And, in fact, that is precisely what has happened. True to the prophetic imagery of messianic fulfillment, the author of Acts sees Mount Zion dripping new wine in the outpouring of the Spirit. We are to drink blood like wine (Zechariah 10:15). We are to drink of the Holy Spirit (1 Corinthians 12) which is the lifeblood of the body of Christ and the new wine filling a new wineskin.

It is just as easy finding scriptural words in praise of wine as in condemnation of drunkenness. Words of wisdom from Sirach or Proverbs assure us that wine in moderation is a demonstration of our creator's loving kindness, but wine in excess is "headaches, bitterness and disgrace" (Sirach 31:29). We know about the disease of alcoholism; this knowledge ought to temper any words of praise for wine. But when Noah got drunk, our scriptures tell us that the sin lay not in his stupor but in the ridicule of Noah's sober son.

Wine is the very life of humanity if taken in moderation. Can someone really live who lacks the wine which was created for our joy? Joy of heart, good cheer and merriment are wine drunk freely at the proper time! (Sirach 31:31)

What happens here? Many more people enter into a longer procession. Communion takes no longer, of course, for the time is controlled by how many go to communion. The people in the front of the center section still have only a very short procession, but it comes at the very end and the whole sense of procession has been established. This procession begins by embracing the whole assembly, as it were, in its movement to the back and then up the center aisle.

We can make this study of Plan A more difficult by moving the outside walls in a little bit and eliminating the aisles on the far sides. This too is a very typical plan. What happens? Some confusion among the people in the side sections when they return to their pews, but no more than happens in the typical "shortest distance" situation. Pews that can

---

ALTAR WINES

"Sacramental wines" are not taxed. Isn't that a simple definition? (During Prohibition only wines labeled "sacramental" were legal.) Any ordinary table wine "from the fruit of the grape" (Canon 924.3) will satisfy canonical requirements for eucharist providing no sugar or other flavorings have been added. The choice of wines depends on the selection offered by local suppliers. Buy samples. It may be possible to purchase affordable wines from any liquor store—despite taxes—which are cheaper than wines purchased through religious goods stores. Find a few parishioners willing to do some comparative shopping. Good wine merchants may be all the assistance you need; it's in their best interest to be of service, and it's grand fun sampling their wares.

In choosing a wine from a liquor store or supplier, check the label to be certain there are no additives (such as sugar or alcohol as described above).

Vary the wine with the seasons. Shouldn't Lent have a different flavor than Eastertime? Gaining a

respect for the wine of eucharist can include informing everyone, through the parish bulletin perhaps, of what sort of wine they're drinking at Mass.

We have made much of the significance of red wine, but most red wines may be too strong. The eucharistic wine should be a variety that is suitably drunk in the morning. That would exclude most full-bodied wines. Experiment with lighter-bodied reds, such as Beaujolais, Burgundy, certain Zinfandels, Gamay, Riojas—and their American equivalents.

A liter (slightly more than a quart) of wine will usually be enough for about 150 people to take a sip, but this can vary widely. Have one parishioner keep a record of the consumption of both bread and wine at the various weekend Masses. A month's experience is enough time to iron out problems and get a good sense of patterns. Use these records to estimate standing bread and wine orders and the quantities needed for extraordinary events. But be alert to what is by now the common experience: As people get used to the presence of the cup each Sunday, more

be entered from one side only will always cause this confusion. It does not affect at all the reasons why a more elaborate procession is desirable.

Plan B, without the little bend in the benches or pews, is very common in older churches. The usual manner of the procession would have the first persons to communion be the ones to the inside of the front pew. They reenter the pew from the other side. Again, only the very last people to communion join in anything like a procession.

The better approach here could be as simple as beginning the procession with the persons to the inside of the back pew (■). They would come forward in the center aisle and return by the side aisles. The people in the front pew would be the last to join in the procession. Everyone would move exactly the same distance as in the more common

and more of them will share it—meaning the amount of wine needed will increase.

Keep wine cool. Lukewarm wine can be unpleasant. Every sacristy needs a refrigerator for opened bottles and to chill the flagons of wine. If they are chilled thoroughly beforehand, they'll stay at drinkable temperatures during Mass, although condensation on the flagons can be a problem.

If your parish is not yet accustomed to sharing the cup, you might be thinking of what to say to people who puzzle over logistics, worry over the cost or fear diseases or alcoholism or a thousand and one other concerns about wine. In point of fact, we seem to have gotten rather sophisticated in imagining complicated excuses for not sharing the cup at every Mass. There are a few, spare words given to us by the Lord Jesus which address these excuses: "Take this, all of you, and drink." These words are simple, blunt and not likely to be misunderstood.

Wine can be both a delight and a danger. We know this from its daily use and surely that is part of its holy use. In wisdom it brings selflessness and cama-raderie, yet in foolishness it brings recklessness and delusion. It is a token of the death of the martyred, like lifeblood flowing from that which is crushed. And yet it is a token of our life in the Spirit, becoming invisibly transformed and capable of inebriating joy. It is nourishment, refreshment and even medicine. Wine is the fruit of the vine and the work of many, many human hands. Surely it is the property of all the baptized who, Sunday after Sunday, need and deserve its holiness at our table.

Vine of heaven, thy blood supplies
this blest cup of sacrifice;
'tis thy cross our healing gives,
to thy cross we look and live.
Thou our life, O let us be
rooted, grafted, grown in thee.

—*Josiah Conder, 1789–1855*

Excerpts from "Wine," by Peter Mazar. Reprinted from *Liturgy 80*, August/September 1987, pp. 7–10.

way of doing communion in this plan, but something is gained: At the beginning, when it is needed, there could be that sense of procession, of the room in movement together, of a common deed.

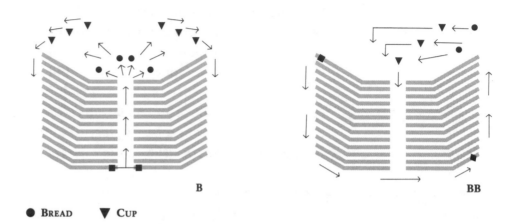

● BREAD ▼ CUP

When the room is small and the numbers fewer, a more elaborate but still workable plan (Plan BB) would have the communion ministers all stationed on one side. Say they take their positions to the right side of the altar. The ushers begin the procession with those in the front pew on the left side (■). These people (and the other pews follow in turn) walk back the side aisle, across the back of the room and come up the side aisle on the right side. They divide to approach the ministers at their stations and from there return to their pews via the center aisle. When the last people from the left side have entered the procession, the ushers begin the right side with the rear pew (◆). People here go out into the side aisle, to the front, back the center aisle and into the pew. Again, for the very last people (those in front on the right side), there is very little procession, but they have been held "within" the procession for the whole time.

Plan C is typical of floor plans with no center aisle. This is very difficult when there are only the three sections. About the only improvement is to take the same approach as in Plan B, treating each section as a separate unit and beginning in the back, using some aisles only for movement forward, some only for movement back.

The Communion Procession

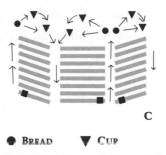

C

● BREAD   ▼ CUP

Plan D resembles Plan C but there are seven sections. This is typical of many new buildings; the number of sections may go even higher than seven. The solution here may be to treat each section as a unit with its own communion ministers. This requires a large number of ministers, but if the room is large and full, this is to be expected. As suggested above, a difference can be made here by beginning from the back and coming forward. This type of arrangement, however, can be viewed in larger groupings of the sections. Plan DD, for example, would require fewer ministers. Any four adjacent sections could be treated as in

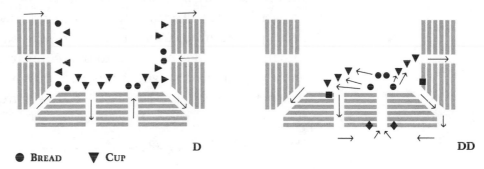

D   DD

● BREAD   ▼ CUP

Plan AA above, giving a full communion procession. At Masses that are not filled, the assembly would always fill these sections first (something that recommends itself for many other reasons). When one or more of the other three sections are filled, these could have their own team of communion ministers and the procession would begin with the people in the pews furthest from the altar. When these sections are only partially filled, the ushers can devise a regular way to lead these people into the one procession.

There are contemporary plans even more complex than any of these, but nearly all would lend themselves to a richer form of procession than the shortest-distance plan.

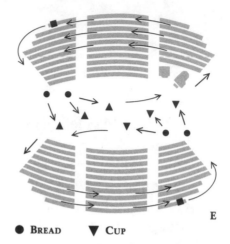

● BREAD ▼ CUP

There has been an increasing number of renovations and of new buildings where the assembly arranges itself in two sections, longer than they are deep, facing each other across the area where the lectern and altar are placed (Plan E). It is easy to see that a true procession is possible in such a space if each long row enters into the movement together, all moving to one end and then into the center area, to the communion ministers who stand throughout this area, then back into the row, so that the first person now follows the last. The row in front then joins in and so on.

PREPARING A PROCESSION

*I*t is best to face two facts from the start: How much depends on the sense and spirit of this procession done well every Sunday. And how you really can't explain this to people. They have to experience being part of a procession.

Everyone involved with the design and execution of the parish's communion procession will say at first that it isn't worth it, that it will be too much trouble and too complicated. It will be trouble. It will be complicated, especially if it is done right. But when it is done, it will be done week after week and it will become "the way we always do it." There will be no thought at all of the complexity, of the failure to move the shortest distance between two points.

Catechesis is vital. If the liturgy is to belong to the assembly, then the assembly is approached with respect. This catechesis would develop an understanding of and a love for the liturgy of the eucharist as a whole so that the need to express our identity as church in these moments of communion would be felt by all. The complexity of changing a pattern for the communion procession should not be underestimated. Ushers and ministers of communion must be prepared not only with instructions but with understanding and enthusiasm. The ushers especially need to manifest a love for the community and for their sharing at the table that goes far beyond hospitality. Those who have chosen to serve as ushers often have this love in abundance, shown through their dependable service and their kindness.

In working out a design for the parish communion procession, the number and placement of the communion ministers is essential. In the better plans, there will be a sense of the entire body caught up in a single procession (as with Plan AA). Here the communion ministers are not serving a single section. Instead, they are grouped so that one or the other may be approached by the communicants as they reach the open area in front of the benches or pews. When the space allows for this, it will often be better to have the ministers of the cup located slightly behind the ministers of bread so that people will not have to cut in front of one another. This placement takes much thought and walking through.

A team of communion ministers serving a given section of the assembly is less pleasing. A quiet sense of separation is bound to settle in, a sense related to the efficiency that seems the first concern. In the design and renovation of worship spaces, the seating arrangement of the assembly should be one of the primary concerns—and this matter of the communion procession should be thought out in every proposed arrangement of chairs or benches.

In all cases, the number of communion ministers will depend on the size of the assembly and the space available for the ministers.

Bread for Each Mass

What do the documents on the liturgy say about whether bread should be taken from the tabernacle for communion at Mass? The *Constitution on the Sacred Liturgy*, said this in 1964:

> That more complete form of participation in the Mass by which the faithful, after the priest's communion, receive the Lord's body *from the same sacrifice*, is strongly endorsed. (no. 55, emphasis added).

The *General Instruction of the Roman Missal*, a few years later, spoke of the breaking of the bread as a preparation for the people's communion:

> Since the eucharistic celebration is the paschal meal, it is right that the faithful who are properly disposed receive the Lord's body and blood as spiritual food as he commanded. *This is the purpose of the breaking of the bread.* . . . In apostolic times this gesture of Christ at the last supper gave the entire eucharistic action its name. This rite is not simply functional, but is a sign that in sharing in the one bread of life which is Christ we who are many are made one body. . . . The priest then shows the eucharistic bread *for communion* to the faithful. . . . (no. 56, emphasis added)

To say that the rite is "not simply functional" is not to deny that it is functional. In fact, it cannot be that "sign" until it is functional. When bread is broken precisely for its sharing, the deed can embody how the many are one. The text continues with words that are crucial to parish practice:

> It is most desirable that the faithful receive the Lord's body from hosts consecrated at the same Mass and that, in the instances when it is permitted, they share in the chalice. Then even through the signs communion will stand out more clearly as a sharing in the sacrifice actually being offered. (no. 56)

That last sentence probably gets as close as anything written to saying *why*—all these years into the reform—it is tragic that the absence is not felt by more ministers and more people. It certainly is clear: We are not talking about rubrical niceties nor monastic ideals, but about simple Christian behavior, basic Christian existence.

There is another sentence in the *General Instruction* that presumes the accepted practice in a parish will be to use only bread consecrated at the Mass being celebrated. The text says this about "articles to be prepared":

> On a side table . . . a paten and ciboria, if needed, with the bread for the communion of the ministers and the people . . . unless all of these are brought in by the faithful at the presentation of the gifts. (no. 80)

Note that the *General Instruction* simply assumes good practice here, even that all the bread is on a single plate and that other containers (ciboria) will be used only if the one large plate cannot hold all the bread needed.

Some additional notes appear in the 1973 text, *Holy Communion and the Worship of the Eucharist outside Mass.* That document speaks first of the ways in which Christ is present in the celebration of Mass: in the assembly, in the word, in the eucharistic elements. Precisely for this reason, "it is more

When the space allows and the numbers would justify it, more rather than fewer ministers can make a difference in the flow of the procession, breaking down that sense of just lining up. This is not to argue for confusion ("Should I go this way or that? To this minister or that one?"). There is always some best number so that each communicant can feel both movement in the procession and rest in the moments of communion. Again, the designs for renovations and new buildings need to allow for this.

The parish plan also needs to take into account the plan for giving communion to persons in wheelchairs when it is difficult for them to approach the usual communion stations, to persons with walkers or to anyone who finds it difficult to enter into the procession. Should a minister go to these people before going to the regular station or at the end of the procession? Beyond the "when" is the "how." Do the ministers understand how to approach these persons with care and respect? Has the parish made it as simple as possible for persons who have a difficult time with the procession? Do they know where special seating (with adequate room) is located? Do they know whom to tell that they wish to receive communion? Do family members and friends feel welcome to assist them in joining in the procession if this is their wish?

---

in keeping with the nature of the celebration that, through reservation of the sacrament in the tabernacle, Christ not be present eucharistically from the beginning on the altar where Mass is celebrated. That presence is the effect of the consecration and should appear as such" (no. 6). The good sense in this last statement is clearly contradicted when the tabernacle regularly becomes a source of bread for holy communion. In fact, the document then notes that consecrated hosts are to be reserved simply "in a number sufficient *for the communion of the sick and of others outside Mass*" (no. 7, emphasis added).

Period. The reservation of hosts is not in any way connected to the use of those hosts at a later Mass.

Is this to say that liturgical wonders will happen if the rubrics are followed and bread for communion is always consecrated at that Mass? That is foolish. But it is not foolish to assert that until it simply *goes without saying* that such things are done, we can have little progress toward the vital liturgy envisioned by the *Constitution* and needed by us all.

Excerpts from "Many Other Things," by Gabe Huck. Reprinted from *Liturgy 80*, January 1986, pp. 8–9.

Another matter concerns the plan for the communion of the musicians. What is not acceptable is for the choir and organist to begin the communion procession if this means that the communion song cannot begin until partway through the procession. Situations vary, but it should be possible to arrive at a plan that allows for the cantor alone or the instrumentalist and cantor to handle all of the leadership at the communion song. The choir members will participate in the same way as other members of the assembly so they can join in the procession at any point. Special measures to bring communion to a choir loft are rarely a good idea. When the choir occupies one area of the assembly's seating, that area can be treated like any other in setting up communion stations. When the choir replaces the cantor in the leadership role, alternating

Bread Recipe

1. For 70 communicants, use ⅓ cup whole wheat flour to ⅔ cup unbleached white flour. The mixture of flour should be kept in an airtight container in the freezer and used while cold. (The cold flour helps prevent a separate crust from forming.)

2. Use one cup of the flour mixture to approximately ½ cup of spring water (Perrier is good). The water should be refrigerator cold.

3. Quickly mix the flour and water together with a fork until all the flour is moist. Form dough into a smooth ball. Usually more flour needs to be sprinkled on the surface of the dough to prevent stickiness.

4. Gently flatten the ball of dough into a circular loaf about ½- to ¾-inch thick. If necessary, turn any uneven edges underneath.

5. Place the unscored loaf on a lightly oiled baking sheet. (I use Pam and wipe off any excess.)

6. Place in a preheated oven at 425°.

7. After approximately 12 to 15 minutes the top crust should have raised slightly. Prick the crust with a toothpick in several places, turn the loaf over and continue to bake about five minutes. (This gives an evenness to the top of the loaf.)

8. Turn loaf right side up again and continue to bake until the crust is very lightly browned, about 10 to 15 minutes more for a total of 25 to 30 minutes. Baking time when using more than 1½ cups of flour needs to be extended.

9. Place the loaf on a rack for cooling. (I usually slice the bottom crust off to check for any rawness.)

10. Bread is best when made fresh the day of the liturgy. However, after cooling it can be tightly wrapped and frozen for later use.

"Bread Recipe," by Dennis Krouse. Reprinted from *Liturgy 80*, October 1986, p. 12.

with the assembly, this can be planned for before or after the members receive communion. When there is a choir but no cantor (a most unhappy situation), the choir can be divided so that some are always able to take part in the song.

It is nearly always possible for the cantor to receive communion at some point, allowing the assembly and instrumentalist to continue with the singing of the refrain alternating with instrumental music. In many cases an organist will be present for more than one liturgy. The organist can receive communion at that liturgy when it is most possible for cantor or choir to continue unaccompanied with the assembly.

Some situations should be avoided: for example, an entire choir coming to communion after everyone else in the assembly has finished

Communion in the Hand

- Communion in the hand should show, as much as communion on the tongue, due respect toward the real presence of Christ in the eucharist. For this reason emphasis should be laid, as was done by the Fathers of the church, upon the *dignity of the gesture of the communicant.* Thus, the newly baptized at the end of the fourth century were directed to stretch out both hands making "the left hand a throne for the right hand, which receives the King." (The *BCL Newsletter* editor notes that "in practice the opposite direction has been given to the faithful: The left hand is to be placed upon the right hand, so that the sacred host can be conveyed to the mouth with the right hand." Certainly, the throne image is intact.)

- Again following the teaching of the Fathers, insistence is to be laid upon the importance of the *Amen*

said in response to the formula of the minister "the Body of Christ"; this *Amen* is an affirmation of the faith. . . .

- It is from the church that the faithful receive the holy eucharist, which is communion in the body of the Lord and in the church; for this reason the communicant should not take from the paten or container, as would be done with ordinary bread, but the hands must be stretched out to receive from the minister of communion.

- Out of respect for the eucharist, cleanliness of hands is expected. Children may need to be reminded of this.

Excerpts from the May 1985 notification from the Congregation for Divine Worship on the subject of communion in the hand, as printed in the *BCL Newsletter*, June/July 1985.

the procession or a communion minister trying to move in and out among various instrumentalists to bring them communion.

With some clarity about what is desired and some imagination, every difficulty about the communion of the musicians can be resolved. Poor practices here can undermine all the other efforts with the communion rite.

WHEN TO BEGIN THE PROCESSION

With any plan for the order of the procession there is the question of when it should begin. If the parish is committed to having the communion ministers in place when the words of invitation are spoken, then such a procession should begin during the singing of the Lamb of God. It should not begin during the very first words of the Lamb of God because here attention should be on the presider and the breaking

Validity of the Bread

The requirements for the validity of the eucharistic bread are rather minimal, notably that the bread be made of wheat and that any additional ingredients do not substantially alter its nature as wheat bread. The requirements for complete liceity are greater in number and more specific. The Code of Canon Law, canon 924, 2, states that the bread must be *merely* wheat and recently baked so that there is no danger of corruption. Canon 926 states that the bread must be unleavened in accord with the ancient tradition of the church. Additional requirements for liceity are found in the *General Instruction of the Roman Missal*, nos. 282–85.

Liturgical law states that the bread must truly have the appearance of food and should be made in such a way that in a Mass with a congregation the priest is able actually to break it into parts and distribute them to at least some of the faithful. It also says that when the number of communicants is large or other pastoral needs require it, small hosts may be used. Finally, care must be taken so that the bread does not spoil or become too hard so that it is difficult to break it.

These requirements of the liturgical law are also for liceity only and they must somehow be harmonized with the directive that the bread be merely wheat with no additives. However, it has been very difficult in practice to discover a recipe for bread that is composed of water and flour only, yet looks like real food.

Excerpt from "Bread and Wine," by John Huels. Reprinted from *Emmanuel*, November 1984. Used with permission.

> *This communion is a <u>procession</u>. This is a banquet to which we have been called not as individuals but as the church.*

of the bread. But when the breaking continues and the litany continues, the ushers could come forward and begin the procession.

THE COMMUNION SONG

The procession depends on the song as much as it depends on the manner of the communion ministers and the choreography of the assembly's movement.

We have noted previously that the song is to begin immediately after the words of invitation. Notes about the nature of this song will be found also in the supplementary materials on pages 17 and 18.

No books should be necessary. The words and music for the communion song should be available to those who want or need them (in the hymnal or on a card or other participation aid). But the nature of the event (a procession in which the hands will be used to take the holy bread and to take the cup) dictates music that the assembly can sing by heart. And it dictates music to process with.

It does not necessarily dictate music that is *about* communion, about the eucharist in a specific way. Some communion music may have this quality, but it is not at all necessary that the words be filled with specific references to bread and wine, body and blood. In fact, the long tradition of the church has been to sing antiphons and psalms with the communion procession. These were not "about" communion in any obvious sense at all. As happens so often, there is great potential in the way these words can then interact with the rite. The psalms remain the primary repertory for the communion song. Other worthy music and words come from the church's tradition and from contemporary composers and poets. What we are looking for in text and melody is music for the paschal banquet, the marriage supper of the lamb where the poor eat and are filled.

A parish does not need a very large number of communion songs: one or two for Advent and Christmastime, two or three for Lent and Eastertime, five or six for Ordinary Time. Seasonal music in the communion song is part of the church's tradition (singing the communion antiphons that went with the feast or season) and much good music exists for this purpose. Probably a parish's first emphasis should be on acquiring a basic in-season-and-out repertory of good music: psalms with refrains, other types of songs or chants with a repeated part for the assembly, chants of the kind made popular by the music of Taizé, gospel music with its own patterns of participation by the assembly.

Another consideration in gathering a parish repertory has to do with how we sing this music: We sing it *in procession*. Sometimes people will be singing in their places but stop when they get into the aisles. What kind of music will we want to go on singing while we walk? That, in fact, is what should bind together the communion procession and song: Singing people walk by me while I am singing and, singing, I walk by singing people. That is a strong part of this rite.

Normally any communion music will involve a cantor or choir singing the changing words while the assembly sings the chorus or refrain. The choir is not to take over the communion music or dominate the assembly's part of the song. People need to feel that the song depends on them. Given adequate musical leadership by the organist or other instrumentalist, people will sing with enthusiasm. Given the limited repertory, it is not necessary to announce the communion song.

THE ASSEMBLY'S PROCESSION

We have these four important elements for the habitual way a parish does the communion procession:

- the presence and manner of the communion ministers
- a plan of movement that allows for a true procession
- a time to begin the procession
- song appropriate to the procession

To those goals the appropriate persons (pastor, staff, musicians, sacristan, communion ministers) dedicate themselves through example, preparation of ministers and catechesis of the whole assembly. This latter has to do with preparing the people for the liturgy. Regarding the communion procession, several aspects of the assembly's role need attention.

Is the assembly to stand or kneel during the invitation? To be standing and attentive would seem appropriate. But then what? Once the communion begins, are people to sit or kneel or remain standing? And what posture for those who return from communion? Decisions should be based on the sense people have for this time and on the postures that will enhance this communion as the community's paschal supper. Often the parish practice reflects uncertainty about these moments. There may

Communion Stations

Ideally there should be sufficient space in the altar area for all communion stations—each station with one minister of the plate and then, at some distance behind, two ministers of cups—so that the feeling generated by the manner of sharing in holy communion is one of approaching the altar, the common holy table, and returning from it. The idea is for the congregational procession(s) to flow toward that focus and then back from it. It may be quite impossible in some buildings, but the experience is worth considerable effort. The contrary experience—of scattering to different corners of the building for communion—is not at all helpful.

There should be a credence table, in a convenient and inconspicuous place, of sufficient size to hold all vessels, utensils and other objects used in the course of the celebration (e.g., nothing is placed on the altar except things actually being used and only for the time they are being used), and where the unconsumed elements can be placed and covered after communion.

Excerpts from "Pastoral Guidelines," by Robert W. Hovda. Reprinted from *It Is Your Own Mystery*, p. 17. Copyright © 1977, The Liturgical Conference, Washington, D.C. All rights reserved. Used with permission.

be a song, but no real sense that everyone is to sing. The kneeling to standing to moving to kneeling or sitting looks like a somewhat public gesture surrounded by private praying.

Sitting most often conveys receptivity, listening, reflection. Yet, at meals, sitting is a posture that conveys engagement—and this is our eucharistic meal. Kneeling conveys adoration and penitence. Standing may be many things, but certainly it is an active attention to and participation in the moment. The decision to remain standing during the time of communion would not be wise if the time for communion were quite long. However, given the presence of ministers of communion, the length of the communion time is fairly independent of the size of the assembly. A small assembly with two communion ministers or a very large assembly with two dozen should take about the same amount of time. If that is so, then standing is an option for this time. It puts those who have finished the procession and those who wait to join it in unity with those in the procession. It gives a communal and public meaning to the whole time so that it can indeed be a fitting home for the most personal moment of the liturgy, the taking of bread and cup by each individual. When there are fewer ministers of communion than the ideal, making the procession time habitually long, then a choice of kneeling or sitting may be necessary. But even here, a common practice does much to demonstrate the nature of these moments.

What about posture in the communion procession? At one time, that was easy. Everyone came forward with folded hands. Today, the variety of postures in the procession reflects our weak sense for what is happening. There is certainly no one right posture, but it should be possible to suggest in catechesis that one's posture deserves care and that even in such a little matter we are to support one another and witness to one another. Coming forward and returning with hands folded is perfectly proper: The gesture conveys attention and focus. Arms at the sides may also be reverent, though it can appear as casual. Walking forward with the hands already in the "throne" position (the right hand cupped under the left, forming a throne for the bread) is another possibility; this speaks of the readiness and even eagerness for the paschal meal. A parish that is serious about building the communion rite may well offer the suggestion of this common posture in the procession forward.

Posture relates also to the attention and focus each person has in the procession: how we walk, where the eyes are fixed (or wandering), participation in the song. Even the best of postures sends a mixed message when a person is not taking part in the song but keeps the lips closed and seems miles away from the rest of the assembly.

To observe people receiving communion leads to a deep curiosity about the meaning of this eating and drinking. Some barely break stride. Some do not look at all at the minister. Some pause to place the bread in the mouth while others do this as they walk toward the cup or back to the procession. Some make the sign of the cross immediately after taking the bread. Some take the cup in their hands, others wait for the minister to raise the cup and give them a drink. To suggest that something else is possible is not to suggest an assembly line with everyone doing exactly the same thing in the same way.

Catechesis in the homily at appropriate times can stress how important each member of the assembly is within this procession. It is good to discuss the practicalities:

• to stop before the minister of the bread with the hands in the throne position (unless one is receiving on the tongue)

The Presider's Communion

The hierarchy is itself of the sacramental order; it is a sign of the church as being a body with different members, in which God has willed to make use of human beings in the service of the community. That is the sole meaning of the hierarchical order. Here again is John Chrysostom, bishop of Constantinople, stressing this point.

I do not have a greater share in the Lord's table and you a lesser; we participate equally. I come first; what difference does that make? Among children, the eldest is the first to reach for the food, but does not get a larger share. . . . I do not receive from one Lamb, you from another; we all share together in the one Lamb.

Excerpts from *The Eucharist* by Robert Cabié; vol. 2 of *The Church at Prayer: An Introduction to the Liturgy*, p. 119. Copyright © 1986, The Order of St. Benedict, Collegeville, Minnesota. All rights reserved. Used with permission.

Amen

In the intensely communal atmosphere created by the Our Father, the kiss of peace, the fraction, and the processional song, an eminently personal action takes place, as each believer approaches the Lord and professes faith in the eucharist. St. Ambrose writes: "Not without reason do you say 'Amen,' for you acknowledge in your heart that you are receiving the body of Christ. When you present yourself, the priest says to you, 'The body of Christ,' and you reply 'Amen,' that is, 'It is so.' Let the heart persevere in what the tongue confesses."

The act of receiving also represents a commitment to live in conformity with the reality that one confesses. St. Augustine makes this point to those whom he has just finished baptizing:

If you are the body and members of Christ, then what is laid on the Lord's table is the sacrament *(mysterium)* of what you yourselves are, and it is the sacrament of what you are that you receive. It is to what you yourselves are that you answer "Amen," and this answer is your affidavit. Be a member of Christ's body, so that your "Amen" may be authentic.

Excerpts from *The Eucharist* by Robert Cabié; vol. 2 of *The Church at Prayer: An Introduction to the Liturgy,* p. 118. Copyright © 1986, The Order of St. Benedict, Collegeville, Minnesota. All rights reserved. Used with permission.

- to look at the minister while being addressed, "The body of Christ"

- to answer, still looking at the minister, with a strong "Amen"

- to raise the hands to receive the bread

- to step to the side, without hurry, and reverently to take the bread and place it in the mouth, then to move toward the minister of the cup

- again to stop before the minister and look at the minister while being addressed, "The blood of Christ," and to answer with a strong "Amen"

- to reach out and take the cup firmly and bring it to one's lips before tipping it and taking a small sip

- to place the cup firmly back in the hands of the minister, without hurry

- to rejoin the procession, perhaps with hands folded together, ready also to join again in the song that gives expression to our solidarity at this table

- to think about "custody of the eyes" during this time (and thus avoid turning the communion into people-watching time)

When people return to their places, we can see at once whether there is a sense for the Lord's supper at which we are all guests—or a sense for a private devotion. Eucharistic piety is a piety of common praise and thanksgiving around the Lord's table. It is personal in every sense of that word. But it is not separate, not private. Eucharistic piety knows and needs a range of expressions, but its very foundation is gone when that range of expressions happens at once. The need to reflect in quiet, to withdraw a bit from communal singing and movement, is a good part of our piety and our rite. This comes after the whole of the communion procession, not just my own communion. It will only be reasonable to ask communicants to remain a part of the rite through singing and attention when they know that these moments will be followed by moments of silence throughout the room, moments in which one can kneel or sit and be still and filled with prayer. People need to know that they can expect such a stillness and can expect that it will continue for a long enough time.

THE PRAYER AFTER COMMUNION

WHEN THE PROCESSION has finished, the communion ministers take the vessels to a table at the side. Here these ministers receive communion. The first minister of the bread and the first minister of the cup to return to this table become ministers to the others. Except for these two, all first place their vessels on the table, then approach for communion. Acolytes and lectors and other ministers who do not sit with the assembly also take communion at this time. Congestion can be avoided by having the ministers stand far enough from this table. Finally, these two ministers give the vessels to the last of the communion ministers and these ministers, in turn, give them communion. Except for the presider, every minister receives communion from another minister.

Another plan for the communion of the ministers themselves would have them place their vessels on the side table, then again take places around the altar (as at the breaking of the bread). The last two ministers to return from their stations then take bread and cup to all the others. Some simple plan must be devised for the communion of these two ministers. Such an approach may prolong the time of the communion procession and call unnecessary attention to the communion of the ministers, but it has the advantage of continuing to focus the communion rite around the altar rather than at the side table.

As long as the tabernacle contains adequate bread for the communion of the sick, what remains should be consumed. When this is not possible, the remaining bread is taken to the tabernacle. A small quantity of consecrated wine can also be reserved but only if it is needed for the communion of sick persons who are unable to take communion in the form of the bread (see *Pastoral Care of the Sick*, no. 74). Any remaining wine should be consumed reverently by the ministers. Consecrated wine is never to be poured into the ground or into the sacrarium (see *This Holy and Living Sacrifice*, no. 38).

In some parishes, those who are to take communion to the sick come forward at this time to place the communion bread in the pyx. If these ministers are to be sent to the sick with appropriate words by the presider at the time of the dismissal, they should remain near the table during the silence and prayer after communion.

As they receive communion, the ministers return to their places in the assembly. During communion, the acolytes have placed any vessels left on the altar on this credence table. The rubrics allow that *all* of the vessels may be purified after Mass (GIRM, no. 120). The last two ministers of communion place their vessels on the table and cover them with a clean cloth that has been placed there for this purpose. It is part of the work of communion ministers to return after Mass in order to purify the vessels.

The presider, after the distribution of communion, gives the plate or cup to an acolyte to take to the side table, then goes to the chair. If the assembly is still singing (and, perhaps, standing), the presider stands or sits (depending on the posture of the assembly) and joins in the song. The song would continue through the communion of the ministers. Then the presider sits down and those in the assembly sit also or kneel. Usually this is a time of silence. The sacramentary reads:

> After communion, the priest and people may spend some time in silent prayer. If desired, a hymn, psalm, or other song of praise may be sung by the entire congregation. (GIRM, no. 56)

Song will rarely be chosen for these moments. This is best kept as a time of silent prayer and reflection. That means that all the ministers must

The ministers place
the vessels on the table
and cover them
with a clean cloth.

keep this time also: no turning pages, no moving about. And no haste is necessary. This is a counterpoint to the song and movement of the procession. Even in this silence—in fact, because of this silence—there is a deep sense of a people at prayer together. The length of this silence ought to be fairly consistent from Sunday to Sunday.

There is never a place for a second collection during this part of the liturgy. All collecting of money belongs during the preparation of the table and the gifts.

THE PRAYER AFTER COMMUNION

The silence is concluded by the presider's invitation, "Let us pray." Because a silent time of prayer has come before this invitation, the presider immediately begins the prayer itself.

It is possible to avoid the jack-in-the-box look (sitting for the silence, standing for the prayer, sitting for the announcements, standing for the blessing) if the assembly remains seated (perhaps some are kneeling) for this prayer. The sacramentary says only that the presider stands. One could argue that it would be better for the presider also to be seated, book of prayers on the lap. On the other hand, standing is certainly the right posture for assembly and for presider at these major prayers of the Mass. The "solution" of having the announcements before the prayer, while all are seated, is altogether out of keeping with the flow of the rite itself. The communion needs the conclusion that this prayer brings, then the assembly moves to what should be a discussion of its business and on to the blessing. The best practice of all may be to stand for the prayer after communion and to remain standing for the announcements, keeping the latter always brief.

The sacramentary is removed from the altar by an acolyte during the communion procession. It is brought to the presider for the prayer after communion, then returned to the table at the side.

Usually these prayers are brief and clear. The texts, unfortunately, are not always vigorous in their use of words and their structure. This is the only presidential prayer in the whole of the communion rite. In fact, except for the invitations and the short "Deliver us" text and the semiprivate prayer "Lord Jesus Christ," it is the only text assigned to the presider. It must be so spoken that it brings this communion rite and the whole liturgy of the eucharist to a conclusion. That is seldom a dramatic sort of conclusion. Rather, it is peaceful and grateful. As is proper, this liturgy of the eucharist is concluded by the assembly's "Amen." A pause should follow, separating the concluding rites (announcements, blessing, dismissal) from all that has gone before. If the sacramentary is not needed for the solemn blessing, it can be closed and removed by the acolyte before the presider begins the concluding rites.

AFTERWORD

THE COMMUNION RITE described in these pages makes sense only as part of a total effort for the strength and beauty of parish liturgy. It makes sense only when it is habitual, the normal way that this assembly does its liturgy. The effort here has been to understand and describe what is possible in the present rite. That rite has, in this area as in others, a potential that is seldom realized. Certainly, the full expression of the communion rite of one parish will be somewhat unlike that of another parish. There is not one "best" communion rite, but there are qualities that any worthy celebration of this rite will have. Those qualities are what this book has been about. They are what the rite wants and needs.

The task in the parish is to establish a steady practice that allows the communion rite to be a focus of full, conscious and active participation. The task is to restore this rite to an assembly that will know in its heart and soul and its muscles, too, that in doing these deeds—Lord's Prayer, peace greeting, Lamb of God, communion procession, eating and drinking Christ's body and blood, keeping silence, praying together—we become what we are, the body of Christ. We learn here what it looks like and sounds like and feels like to be that body and so begin little by little to keep on being that way. In the eucharistic prayer and the communion rite we are the baptized (all the catechumens have gone), those who have assembled on the Lord's Day to do once again what is the right and the duty of the baptized. Here we bring our hunger for the reign of God—and that is why we come fasting to this liturgy—and here we are fed with a morsel of the bread of the poor and a sip of the heavenly banquet. Here we have joined ourselves to one another in a broken loaf and common cup, joined ourselves with absolutely none of the world's distinctions. And we have joined in communion also with all the baptized who ever came to this table. In some sense—because baptism makes us not members of a club but nonmembers of every club, thus only human brothers and sisters—we have joined with everyone, facing what evil has made of our world, yet glimpsing and tasting the reign of God.

APPENDIX

The materials on the following pages may be reproduced by purchasers of this book for use in parishes and other institutions. The proper acknowledgment should appear whenever these pages are duplicated.

Sample Instructions for Communion Ministers

ARRIVAL

Sign in 15 minutes before the Mass in the Sunday sacristy just to the right of the entrance vestibule. The sign-in form is either on the bulletin board or with the team leader. (At each station, the "first minister of the cup" stands closest to the minister of the bread.)

Join the other liturgical ministers in the vestibule or on the church steps to greet parishioners as they arrive. When the tower bell rings—five minutes before Mass—take your place wherever you wish in the church.

Unassigned ministers are asked to stop by the Sunday sacristy when the tower bell rings to see if they are needed as substitutes.

BEFORE COMMUNION

During the sign of peace, greet others as you come forward to the altar.

The Pouring and Cup Ministers come up to the right side of the altar (as they face it). The Bread Ministers come up to the left side of the altar (as they face it).

After the breaking of the bread, the Pouring Minister brings the tray with the cups and purificators to the altar from the credence table and fills all the cups from the flagon. The presider moves the flagon of wine over so that it is closer to the Pouring Minister. The assigned minister brings the empty plate(s) from the credence table to the altar. This minister remains at the altar and assists the presider in breaking the bread and filling the plates.

Cup Ministers come forward one at a time, taking their cups as they are filled. Each takes a purificator also and goes directly to his or her communion station.

Ministers of the bread come forward one at a time, take a plate and go to their stations.

The Cup Ministers should be positioned facing the Bread Minister (at their station) so that people taking the cup will not block the flow of other communicants. Leave enough space between ministers to accommodate waiting communicants.

When all cups have been filled and taken, the Pouring Minister steps back from the altar.

When all ministers are in their places, the presider says, "This is the Lamb of God . . ."

All ministers face the presider until after the "Lord, I am not worthy . . . ," then they face the assembly.

COMMUNION

After the response, "Lord, I am not worthy . . . ," the presider takes communion. Then the presider and the one Cup Minister who has remained at the altar take the plate and chalice and go to the two open stations. The presider should take the cup as often as the bread. Meanwhile, the communion of the assembly has begun.

If, as a Cup Minister, you run out of wine, simply place the empty cup on the credence table and wait there to receive communion.

If you finish at your station and have bread or wine remaining, look to see if anyone else still has a long line. If this is the case, go and assist at that station.

RECEPTION OF COMMUNION BY MINISTERS

The Ministers who finish distributing communion first go to a position near the cre-dence table to give communion to the other ministers.

The Bread Minister stands facing the assembly. The Cup Minister stands at the left of the Bread Minister.

As the other ministers finish distributing communion they return and place cup or plate on the credence table, then get in line to receive communion. After communion, they return to their place in the assembly.

Finally, those who have been distributing to the other ministers give plate and cup to the last two receiving communion so that they themselves can receive. These four should consume the remaining wine and bread. If there is too much bread for this, one minister takes it to the tabernacle.

AFTER MASS

The Pouring Minister and the minister who assisted with the breaking of the bread remove the vessels from the credence table and assist the sacristan in purifying them at the sacrarium.

Adapted from the instructions prepared by St. Clement Church, Chicago.

Sample Questions and Answers for Eucharistic Ministers

What if I forget my station or go to the wrong place?

Stay calm. It's happened before. Just look around to see where the gap is. Then walk over there.

So I've found my communion station, which way do I face?

First, face the presider from "This is the Lamb of God . . ." until after you have responded, "Lord, I am not worthy . . ." Then, ministers of the bread face the assembly and ministers of the cup face their minister of the bread.

What if I get to my station and realize that I've forgotten my purificator?

Just calmly go back to the altar and get one.

Or, a worse situation: What if I drop the purificator and there isn't one left on the altar?

There will be extra purificators on the credence table.

What about dropped bread? Spilled wine?

If the bread is dropped, pick it up and keep it separate from the ones you are giving to people. Afterwards, put it on the credence table. If you do not wish to consume it yourself, mention it to the team leader. If wine is spilled, put your purificator down to soak it up. If you need another purificator, extras are on the credence table. Tell the sacristan after Mass.

What about communicants who want to dip their bread in the cup?

BARBARA SCHMICH

The liturgy directives discourage this practice because it does not fully express the meaning "take and drink," yet some prefer this. We are glad to share communion with them. Remember to hold the cup securely because they will not take it.

If my station is finished, should I help distribute communion somewhere else?

If the lines are long, go where you can be of assistance.

What do we do with the leftover consecrated bread and wine?

First, place your vessel on the credence table and receive communion the usual way. If it is clear that there is an extra quantity of bread or wine, the ministers can help to consume

99

this in their own communion. If any bread still remains, it is taken to the tabernacle by the designated minister. If you are so designated, take the vessel and place it in the tabernacle. Try to do so without calling attention to yourself. If wine still remains, the ministers should consume all of it.

What do I do with my purse and other valuables?

We encourage you to leave your purse and valuables in the Sunday church office.

What if I'm scheduled to be a eucharistic minister and I don't show up and I don't get a replacement?

The rest of us really miss you and we run around at the last minute looking over the assembly for someone we recognize as a minister of communion. We do understand that you sometimes cannot be with us, but please get a responsible replacement and give his/her name to your team leader. If you have not signed in when the bells ring (at five minutes before Mass), we will try to find a replacement. Members of other teams are usually quite gracious about helping out. Information about other ministers, with their preferred Mass times, is on the roster. When all else fails, call your team leader or the assistant team leader.

Adapted from material prepared by St. Clement Church, Chicago.

Our Celebration of Communion

EVERY SUNDAY, the Lord's Day, we assemble as a parish community to celebrate the eucharist. We begin with song and greetings and prayers. We spend time in hearing the scriptures and reflecting on how God's word is shaping our lives. We offer intercessions for the world, the poor, the church, all those in need. We then lift up our hearts in praise and thanks to God and we pray that the simple gifts of bread and wine might become for us the body and blood of our Lord, Jesus Christ.

The communion that follows begins with the Lord's Prayer and continues through to the Amen that concludes the prayer after communion. This whole communion time has many different moments, yet it also has a unity. The guidelines which follow are meant to invite you to your full part in communion.

1. Pray the Lord's Prayer vigorously together because it is our treasure, the sum of all our prayer, and because on the Lord's Day we pronounce our prayer as an assembly. No one should doubt that you love these words and that this common recitation is rehearsed at home each morning and night.

2. We were baptized to seek and pray for the peace of Christ. With your gestures, then, and with your words and with your eyes, let Christ's peace be felt and heard and seen as you turn to one another. Here for brief moments is the world-to-come present in our midst: all barriers fallen, God's children making peace. This will not be found in polite handshakes nor in extended socializing. The peace you give and receive is that of those who bear one another's burdens. Only that peace prepares us to approach the Lord's table. Rejoice when, in your assembly, this

BARBARA SCHMICH

peace joins hands of many colors, many ages, many walks of life.

3. Fix your eyes on the one bread as the presider silently raises it and breaks it into pieces for the communion. While the bread is being broken and the wine poured into cups, join in the Lamb of God and sing devoutly this litany for mercy and peace.

4. When all is ready for communion, the presider proclaims the invitation: "Happy are those who are called to his supper." Answer with ancient and true words: "Lord, I am not worthy to receive you, but only say the word and I shall be healed." Invited to the communion are all those present who have been initiated to this table in the Roman Catholic Church and who strive to be at peace with God and seek God's love and justice in the world. In a joyful anticipation of this banquet, fast from other food for at least one hour before approaching this table.

5. Let your song and even the way you move together toward the table show forth the

church, the one body of Christ that you are. Sing songs and psalms and refrains whose very sound will express and make strong this holy communion. Walk in such a way that no one could confuse this procession with a "lining up" of individuals. It is the supper of the Lamb to which this church has been invited: Let there be dignity and grace and eagerness in the processing and singing. It is fitting to walk in the procession with hands folded or with the left hand resting in the right hand. This position of the hands is like making a throne for the body of Christ.

6. This holy communion is encountered as a banquet, the image and promise of God's reign. Eat the simple bread that is Christ's body, drink from the cup that seals our covenant in Christ's blood. Look at the minister of communion and speak a joyful and firm "Amen" when the minister proclaims to you, "The body of Christ," "The blood of Christ." St. Augustine said: "It is your own mystery which you receive. It is to what you are that you reply Amen, and by replying subscribe."

7. After receiving the bread, step to one side and pause for a moment as you reverently place the bread in your mouth.

8. After the minister of the cup says, "The blood of Christ," and you respond, "Amen," take the cup firmly in both hands. Without haste, bring it to your lips and drink. Then reverently return the cup to the hands of the minister.

9. Return in the procession to your place, still singing until the whole procession is completed. When the ministers have returned the vessels to their places, remain in silent prayer and reflection.

10. Listen to the simple prayer which the presider speaks to conclude the communion and say "Amen" to all that has been said and done.

Our Communion, Our Peace, Our Promise

At this table we put aside every worldly separation based on culture, class, or other differences. Baptized, we no longer admit to distinctions based on age or sex or race or wealth. This communion is why all prejudice, all racism, all sexism, all deference to wealth and power must be banished from our parishes, our homes, and our lives. This communion is why we will not call enemies those who are human beings like ourselves. This communion is why we will not commit the world's resources to an escalating arms race while the poor die. We cannot. Not when we have feasted here on the "body broken" and "blood poured out" for the life of the world.

Let that be clear in the reverent way we walk forward to take the holy bread and cup. Let it be clear in the way ministers of communion announce: "The body of Christ," "The blood of Christ." Let it be clear in our "Amen!" Let it be clear in the songs and psalms we sing and the way we sing them. Let it be clear in the holy silence that fills this church when all have partaken.

Before coming forward we say, "Lord, I am not worthy." We are never worthy of this table, for it is God's grace and gift. Yet we do come forward. This is "food for the journey" that we began at baptism. We may eat of it when we are tired, when we are discouraged, even when we have failed. But not when we have forgotten the church, forgotten the way we began at the font; not when we have

abandoned our struggle against evil and remain unrepentant for having done so. Let us examine our lives honestly each time before approaching the eucharist. "Worthy" none of us ever is, but properly prepared each one of us must be. Christ, present in the eucharist and in us, calls us to be a holy communion, to grow in love and holiness for one another's sake.

Excerpt from *Our Communion, Our Peace, Our Promise: Pastoral Letter on the Liturgy*, by Joseph Cardinal Bernardin, Archbishop of Chicago. Copyright © 1984, Archdiocese of Chicago. Liturgy Training Publications, 1800 North Hermitage Avenue, Chicago IL 60622-1101; 312/486-7008.

Communion from the Cup: Part I

EVERY SUNDAY when we pray the eucharistic prayer, we hear these words: "Take this, all of you, and drink from it: this is the cup of my blood." And a few moments later, we are invited: "Happy are those who are called to his supper."

More than 20 years ago, the *Constitution on the Sacred Liturgy* of Vatican II urged that a beginning be made: On some occasions communion should be received in the fullness of the sign, both the bread and the cup.

Encouraged by the United States bishops, communion under both bread and wine may be offered to all at parish Masses on Sundays when the local bishop has authorized this practice.

In his pastoral letter on the liturgy, Joseph Cardinal Bernardin expressed "my encouragement for communion under both kinds as prescribed by liturgical norms." In this he echoed what the Vatican's *General Instruction of the Roman Missal* said in 1969: "It is most desirable that the faithful . . . share in the chalice. Then, even through signs, communion will stand out more clearly as a sharing in the sacrifice actually being offered." And later in the same document we read: "Holy communion has a more complete form as a sign when it is received under both kinds. For in this manner of reception a fuller light shines on the sign of the eucharistic banquet."

Nothing is changed here from the church's teaching that under the form of bread or under the form of wine, Christ—whole and entire—is received. Although you are invited

to receive communion under both forms, everyone retains the option not to do so.

But we are human. We remember what Paul wrote to the Corinthians: "Every time you eat this bread and drink this cup, you proclaim the death of the Lord until he comes." We do things in human ways. What could be more so than this eating and this drinking? In bread, "the staff of life," we find strength and nourishment. In wine, "fruit of the vine and work of human hands," we find delight and festivity and God's promise of salvation.

Communion from the Cup: Part II

COMMUNION FROM THE CUP is encouraged because by both eating and drinking we may join more wholeheartedly in the full celebration of the eucharist.

Eating and drinking, we proclaim the Lord's death until he comes.

Eating and drinking, we show forth the kingdom we await.

Eating and drinking, we realize more and more that we are Christ's. We become the bread broken and the cup poured out for the life of the world.

Some ask about the manner of receiving from the cup. The parish will usually have two ministers of the cup for each minister distributing the consecrated bread. Normally you will first receive the host. Then approach one of the ministers of the cup. When your turn comes, the minister will extend the cup and say to you: "The blood of Christ." You respond firmly, "Amen." Then take the cup securely in both hands, bring it to your lips and drink from it. Do not hurry. This is to be a holy and reverent action. Put the cup back into the minister's hands and return to your place.

The question always arises: Isn't this unhealthy, so many people drinking from one cup? Gerald J. Dorff, MD, writing the *Linacre Quarterly* in 1980, reviewed the research done on this and the medical factors involved. He concluded: "Suffice it to say the strongest argument for continuing the use of the common communion cup is the fact that there has never been a 'point source' outbreak of a communicable disease directly related to the common communion cup."

BARBARA SCHMICH

The Rev. Thomas Welbers, writing in *Our Sunday Visitor* in 1979, made the following points:

—A few diseases infect through direct mouth-saliva-mouth contact, but "During the cold season or flu epidemic the faithful Catholic is more likely to get sick merely by breathing the air in church than by receiving communion from a shared cup."

—The proper procedure of administering the cup will ensure that no infective dose of any pathogen will be transmitted. Thus, after each communion, the minister wipes the cup and turns it for the next recipient.

Finally, what of children? If children first taste wine at the family table and know it as a sign of joy and festivity, and if they learn from their parents' example how to take the cup with reverence, then they too may receive from the cup.

La comunión en la copa: 1ª parte

CADA DOMINGO, cuando rezamos la oración eucarística, escuchamos estas palabras: "Tomad y bebed todos de él, porque éste es el cáliz de mi sangre." Momentos después, recibimos esta invitación: "Dichosos los invitados a la cena del Señor."

Hace más de 20 años, la *Constitución de la Sagrada Liturgia* II introdujo la siguiente adaptación: en ciertas ocasiones la comunión debería recibirse en la plenitud de su signo, en el pan y en la copa.

Muchos de nosotros lo hemos presenciado: la copa se ofrece a todos los que se acercan a comulgar. Los fieles que toman parte en la Misa han aceptado favorablemente y de una forma hermosa esta práctica.

Los obispos de los Estados Unidos han favorecido la comunión bajo las dos especies del pan y del vino para todos los fieles durante la Misa dominical. Hace un año, en su carta pastoral sobre la liturgia, el Cardenal Bernardin de Chicago declaró: "Mi deseo es que se reciba la comunión bajo las dos especies como ha sido ordenado por las normas litúrgicas." La declaración del cardenal subraya las indicaciones de la *Instrucción General del Misal Romano* del Vaticano en 1969: "Es muy de desear que los fieles . . . participen del cáliz, de modo que aparezca mejor, por los signos exteriores, que la comunión es una participación en el sacrificio que entonces mismo se celebra." Más adelante, en el mismo documento leemos: "La comunión tiene una expresión más plena por razón del signo cuando se hace bajo las dos especies. Ya que en esa forma es donde más perfectamente se manifiesta el signo del banquete eucarístico . . ."

BARBARA SCHMICH

Esto no contradice las enseñanzas de la iglesia que dicen que se recibe a Cristo, total y completo, bajo la especie de pan y de vino. De la misma manera, nadie tiene la obligación de recibir la comunión bajo las dos especies: Ud. puede recibir la comunión de la forma que prefiera.

Pero somos humanos. Recordemos que Pablo escribió a los corintios: "Cada vez que coman de este pan y beban de este cáliz, proclamarán la muerte de Nuestro Señor hasta que venga." Nosotros obramos en forma humana. ¿Hay, acaso, algo que nos humanice más que el participar en esta cena? El pan, el "sostén de la vida," nos fortalece y nos enriquece. El vino, "fruto de la viña y trabajo de manos humanas," nos deleita y nos ayuda a celebrar la promesa de salvación.

La comunión en la copa: 2ª parte

LA COMUNIÓN EN LA COPA se favorece en la Misa dominical porque al comer y al beber podemos compartir plenamente en la celebración de la eucaristía.

Al comer y al beber el cuerpo y la sangre del Señor, proclamamos la muerte del Señor hasta que venga.

Al comer y al beber, manifestamos el reino que esperamos.

Al comer y al beber, demostramos más y más que somos de Cristo. Nos convertimos en el pan compartido y en el cáliz derramado por la vida del mundo.

¿Cuál es la manera más apropiada de recibir la copa? La parroquia generalmente tendrá dos ministros de copa por cada ministro que distribuye el pan consagrado. Normalmente Ud. recibirá primero la hostia. Después, acérquese a uno de los ministros de copa. Cuando le toque a Ud., el ministro extenderá la copa y le dirá: "La sangre de Cristo." Usted responderá: "Amén." Luego tome la copa con ambas manos, llévesela a los labios y beba de ella. No se dé prisa. Esta debe ser una acción sagrada y reverente. Ponga la copa otra vez en las manos del ministro, y regrese a su lugar.

¿Es higiénico el que beban tantas personas de la misma copa? ¿No se corre peligro de infección? En 1980, Gerald J. Dorff, MD, documentó en el *Linacre Quarterly* los resultados de las investigaciones que se han hecho al respecto y los factores médicos que les corresponden. Concluyó: "Basta decir que el argumento más fuerte a favor del uso de la copa común es el hecho de que jamás se ha establecido ésta como fuente de infección."

BARBARA SCHMICH

El Padre Thomas Welbero, hizo las siguientes observaciones en *Our Sunday Visitor* en 1979:

—Pocas enfermedades se transmiten por el contacto directo entre la boca—la saliva—la boca, pero más fácil es para un católico contraer un resfriado durante una temporada de gripe al respirar el aire en la iglesia que al compartir la copa.

—Si se administra correctamente la copa, no se transmitirá infecciosa dosis patógena alguna. Por eso, después de cada comunión, el ministro debe limpiar el borde de la copa antes de entregárselo a la persona siguiente.

¿Y los niños? Si se les permite beber vino en la mesa familiar y lo identifican con el gozo y el festejo, y si aprenden por el ejemplo de sus padres a aceptar la copa con reverencia, entonces ellos también podrán recibir la copa.